REGENTS RESTORATION DRAMA SERIES

General Editor: John Loftis

THE CONSCIOUS LOVERS

RICHARD STEELE

The Conscious Lovers

Edited by

SHIRLEY STRUM KENNY

UNIVERSITY OF NEBRASKA PRESS · LINCOLN

Library of Congress Catalog Card Number: 68–11409

MANUFACTURED IN THE UNITED STATES OF AMERICA

Regents Restoration Drama Series

The Regents Restoration Drama Series provides soundly edited texts, in modern spelling, of the more significant plays of the late seventeenth and early eighteenth centuries. The word "Restoration" is here used ambiguously and must be explained. If to the historian it refers to the period between 1660 and 1685 (or 1688), it has long been used by the student of drama in default of a more precise word to refer to plays belonging to the dramatic tradition established in the 1660's, weakening after 1700, and displaced in the 1730's. It is in this extended sense—imprecise though justified by academic custom—that the word is used in this series, which includes plays first produced between 1660 and 1737. Although these limiting dates are determined by political events, the return of Charles II (and the removal of prohibitions against operation of theaters) and the passage of Walpole's Stage Licensing Act, they enclose a period of dramatic history having a coherence of its own in the establishment, development, and disintegration of a tradition.

Some fifteen editions having appeared as this volume goes to press, the series has reached perhaps a third of its anticipated range of between forty and fifty volumes. The volumes will continue to be published for a number of years, at the rate of three or more annually. From the beginning the editors have planned the series with attention to the projected dimensions of the completed whole, a representative collection of Restoration drama providing a record of artistic achievement and providing also a record of the deepest concerns of three generations of Englishmen. And thus it contains deservedly famous plays—*The Country Wife*, *The Man of Mode*, and *The Way of the World*—and also significant but little known plays, *The Virtuoso*, for example, and *City Politiques*, the former a satirical review of scientific investigation in the early years of the Royal Society, the latter an equally satirical review of politics at the time of the Popish Plot. If the volumes of famous plays finally achieve the larger circulation, the other volumes may conceivably have the greater utility, in making available texts otherwise difficult of access with the editorial apparatus needed to make them intelligible.

The editors have had the instructive example of the parallel and senior project, the Regents Renaissance Drama Series; they have in fact used the editorial policies developed for the earlier plays as their own, modifying them as appropriate for the later period and as the experience of successive editions suggested. The introductions to the separate Restoration plays differ considerably in their nature. Although a uniform body of relevant information is presented in each of them, no attempt has been made to impose a pattern of interpretation. Emphasis in the introductions has necessarily varied with the nature of the plays and inevitably—we think desirably—with the special interests and aptitudes of the different editors.

Each text in the series is based on a fresh collation of the seventeenth- and eighteenth-century editions that might be presumed to have authority. The textual notes, which appear above the rule at the bottom of each page, record all substantive departures from the edition used as the copy-text. Variant substantive readings among contemporary editions are listed there as well. Editions later than the eighteenth century are referred to in the textual notes only when an emendation originating in some one of them is received into the text. Variants of accidentals (spelling, punctuation, capitalization) are not recorded in the notes. Contracted forms of characters' names are silently expanded in speech prefixes and stage directions, and, in the case of speech prefixes, are regularized. Additions to the stage directions of the copy-text are enclosed in brackets.

Spelling has been modernized along consciously conservative lines, but within the limits of a modernized text the linguistic quality of the original has been carefully preserved. Contracted preterites have regularly been expanded. Punctuation has been brought into accord with modern practice. The objective has been to achieve a balance between the pointing of the old editions and a system of punctuation which, without overloading the text with exclamation marks, semicolons, and dashes, will make the often loosely flowing verse and prose of the original syntactically intelligible to the modern reader. Dashes are regularly used only to indicate interrupted speeches, or shifts of address within a single speech.

Explanatory notes, chiefly concerned with glossing obsolete words and phrases, are printed below the textual notes at the bottom of each page. References to stage directions in the notes follow the admirable system of the Revels editions, whereby stage directions are keyed, decimally, to the line of the text before or after which they occur.

Thus, a note on 0.2 has reference to the second line of the stage direction at the beginning of the scene in question. A note on 115.1 has reference to the first line of the stage direction following line 115 of the text of the relevant scene. Speech prefixes, and any stage directions attached to them, are keyed to the first line of accompanying dialogue.

JOHN LOFTIS

October, 1967
Stanford University

Contents

List of Abbreviations

O1	First octavo (all copies)
O1(u)	First octavo (uncorrected)
O1(c)	First octavo (corrected)
O2	Second octavo
O3	Third octavo
D1	First duodecimo (1730 "Third Edition")
Dub.	First Dublin edition (1722)
J	T. Johnson's edition (1722, The Hague)
SB	*Studies in Bibliography*
S.D.	stage direction
S.P.	speech prefix

Introduction

On October 20, 1722, eighteen days before *The Conscious Lovers* opened at the Drury Lane Theatre, Sir Richard Steele assigned the publication rights to Jacob Tonson Jr. for £40 and "divers other good Causes and Considerations."[1] Tonson reassigned half of the rights to Bernard Lintot within a week, and on December 1 the play was published with the date 1723 on the title page. The theatrical success of the play, doubtless enhanced by a critical controversy over Steele's concept of comedy, created a great demand for copies; Tonson had "many thousand" printed, and immediately "a good part" of these were sold.[2] The type was tied, stored, and reimposed several times. Corrections were introduced, probably between press-runs. Before the type from this edition had been completely distributed, the need for more copies became evident, and a second edition was printed; undistributed type from the first was used in pages of seven formes. A third, also dated 1723, followed the second. Neither the second nor the third edition, however, was labeled as such; each could easily be mistaken by an unwary reader for the first. No authorial revisions were introduced into either, but a few printers' errors crept in.

The title page of the first edition reads:

> THE/ Conscious Lovers./ A/ COMEDY./ As it is Acted at the/ Theatre Royal in *Drury-Lane*,/ By His MAJESTY's Servants.// Written by/ Sir *RICHARD STEELE.*// [motto]// *LONDON:*/ Printed for J. TONSON at *Shakespear*'s *Head* over-/ against *Katharine-Street* in the *Strand.* 1723.

The title pages of the second and third editions read identically except for one line-division between the fourth and fifth lines of the motto (first edition: *Miseri-/ cordiam*; second and third editions:

[1] Original agreement, now in the Widener Library, quoted in Rodney M. Baine, "The Publication of Steele's *Conscious Lovers*," *SB*, II (1949–1950), 170.

[2] G. A. Aitken, "Steele's 'Conscious Lovers' and the Publishers," *Athenaeum*, December 5, 1891, p. 771, citing Chancery Pleadings, Winter 1714–1758, No. 690.

Misericor-/ diam). All have the same collational formula: 8°: A–F⁸ G⁴. There are differences in line-divisions but only one variation in pagination: the last line of A5ᵛ in the first edition is the first line of A6 in the second and third. A couple of other variants will distinguish the three editions. The first line of page 22 begins "But I" in the first edition and "I" in the second and third; the fourth line of page 29 contains the reading "thing right" in the first and second editions and the misreading "right thing" in the third.[3]

The enormous popularity of the play invited piracies. As early as December 8, a week after publication, Tonson was threatened by an unauthorized edition which he stopped by legal action.[4] Another publisher, however, got his copies into the streets of London by printing abroad: T. Johnson published an octavo with the imprint London and the date 1723; actually it was printed at The Hague, probably in 1722. A duodecimo dated 1722 was printed in Dublin by A. Rhames. Although these copies appeared soon after the original, the number of Tonson's sales, as indicated by the early second and third editions, continued high. No copies labeled second edition ever appeared, but Tonson published a "Third Edition" in 1730, the year after Steele's death. The first served as copy-text for this duodecimo. A reprint of the Dublin edition was issued in 1725.

At least forty-seven editions were printed before the end of the century. In some of the later ones the text is cut as the stage production was, and in some the entire text is printed but the cuts are indicated. Besides the twenty-four published in London, including an Italian translation in 1724, there were three editions in French published in Paris, two in German in Dresden and Leipzig, and one in English in Göttingen. At least sixteen editions appeared in Ireland and Scotland.

For the present text I have collated twelve copies of the first edition, two of the second, two of the third, the 1730 edition, Johnson's dated 1723, and those published in Dublin in 1722 and 1725. Variants in Johnson's and the first Dublin edition are noted only if they unquestionably correct errors and therefore are accepted into this edition.

As Professor John Loftis has shown, it is likely that Steele began

[3] For a bibliographical examination of the three editions and a discussion of the printing history, see my article, "Eighteenth-century Editions of Steele's *Conscious Lovers*," in *SB*, XXI (1968), 253–261.

[4] Aitken, p. 771.

writing *The Conscious Lovers* while he was editing *The Tatler*.[5] He settled down to serious work on his manuscript in 1719 and completed a version which was supposed to be produced in the winter or spring of 1720. The comedy did not reach the stage during that season, though Steele introduced some of the characters and a song from it in his periodical *The Theatre*.

In the fall of 1722 the play finally went into rehearsal at Drury Lane. Steele was then governor of the theater by royal patent. Colley Cibber, one of the partners in the management and the play's first Tom, advised Steele about it, giving "more Assistance . . . than becomes me to enlarge upon,"[6] he later claimed. Steele acknowledged a debt to Cibber for "his care and application in instructing the actors and altering the disposition of the scenes when I was, through sickness, unable to cultivate such things myself."[7] Cibber's son, who played Daniel, rated his father's contribution as far greater; at Steele's request, he said, Cibber had contributed "many additions" and had thereby "greatly improved" the play. It was Cibber, his son said, who had seen that the play was "rather too grave for an English audience" and recommended adding comic characters;[8] Steele allegedly took this suggestion and added the parts of Tom and Phillis, drawing the episode of romantic window-washing from one of his periodical papers, *Guardian*, No. 87.

Many others also read and discussed the comedy before opening night. John Dennis acidly remarked that it was "read to more Persons than will be at the Representation of it, or vouchsafe to read it, when it is publish'd."[9] Rehearsals attracted audiences of "many excellent Judges," who, according to one report, unanimously approved the play.[10] The poet Leonard Welsted wrote the prologue and also an epilogue published with the play. Benjamin Victor wrote the epilogue spoken on the first night.[11]

[5] John Loftis, *Steele at Drury Lane* (Berkeley and Los Angeles, 1952), pp. 184–189.

[6] Colley Cibber, *An Apology for the Life of Mr. Colley Cibber*, ed. R. W. Lowe (London, 1889), II, 206.

[7] The Preface, ll. 64–67.

[8] Theophilus Cibber, *The Lives of the Poets of Great Britain and Ireland* (London, 1753), IV, 120.

[9] John Dennis, *A Defence of Sir Fopling Flutter*, in *The Critical Works of John Dennis*, ed. Edward Niles Hooker (Baltimore, 1943), II, 241.

[10] Letter from "Townly," *St. James's Journal*, November 15, 1722.

[11] This epilogue was printed with the second edition of Victor's laudatory

Excitement about Sir Richard's long-promised comedy was genuine but scarcely spontaneous. Puffs were inserted in the newspapers to suggest that it was "the very best that ever came upon the *English* Stage."[12] Dennis claimed that these paragraphs could have been written by no one but the author, or one of his "zanies" at his instigation.[13] So indignant was Dennis at the success of Sir Richard's publicity campaign that he added to the pre-opening excitement by publishing a pamphlet attacking the play five days before it reached the stage. The subsequent controversy was undoubtedly profitable to Steele, the theater, and the booksellers.

The Drury Lane company staged an elaborate performance. Although Welsted in his prologue condemned attempts to win audiences by "gay show and costly habits," the company prepared new sets and costumes, opulent enough to justify or at least support advanced prices. When no one was found to sing Indiana's love song in Act II, a virtuoso violinist was hired to present a musical interlude.

These lures, added to the promise of a completely new kind of comedy, were enough to draw a full house of fashionable playgoers on opening night, November 7, 1722. According to a newspaper report, "a greater Concourse of People was never known to be assembled."[14] Sir Richard, sitting with friends in Burton's Box, an enclosed section of the gallery, enjoyed what he considered an excellent performance.[15] The audience proved receptive, and *The Conscious Lovers* was immediately a success.

During its first season it brought in £2,536 3*s.* 6*d.*, more money than any play previously performed by the company.[16] To Steele himself, notorious for his financial troubles, it brought more than £1,000,

---

Epistle to Sir Richard Steele, On his Play, call'd The Conscious Lovers (London, 1722) and, with a few variants, in his *Original Letters, Dramatic Pieces, and Poems* (London, 1776), III, 75–76. The anonymous author of *The Censor Censured: or, The Conscious Lovers Examin'd* (London, 1723) suggests that Steele chose to publish a moral epilogue with his play to avoid the "bawdy" one which ridicules Bevil's failure to make better use of his opportunities with Indiana.

[12] *Defence*, in Dennis, *Critical Works*, II, 241.

[13] *Ibid.*

[14] *Daily Journal*, November 8, 1722, quoted in Emmett L. Avery, *The London Stage 1660–1800 Part 2: 1700–1729* (Carbondale, Ill., 1960), II, 694.

[15] Letter to David Garrick, September, 1762, in Victor, *Original Letters*, I, 327–328.

[16] Public Records Office, C11/2416/49. Quoted in Loftis, p. 193.

including a gift of £500 from King George I[17] and profits from his three third-night benefits, his share as a patentee of the theater, and his sale of publication rights. It had a first run of eighteen nights and might have run even longer according to one report, "if, upon other Considerations, the Players had not thought proper to give it a violent Death, without waiting for its natural Expiration."[18]

Critics, even less willing than the players to let the play die a natural death, attacked it savagely. Their motives were sometimes questionable; Dennis, for example, was allegedly vindictive because of the Drury Lane managers' earlier treatment of one of his plays.[19] He and others combined personal attack with critical commentary, and they attacked trivial detail and fundamental dramatic theory with equal vigor. They condemned Steele for the improbability of the incidents, the "affected, impure, and barbarous"[20] diction, the characters, the dialogue, and the sententiousness. More important, they heartily disapproved of his concept of comedy. The one scene that all of them, even Dennis, considered good was Indiana's discovery of her father; their attitude reflects the growing taste for pathos. Steele's supporters defended him in pamphlets and newspapers, and some critics attempted an impartial view, but they could not match the energy of his enemies. The critical war raged for months, long after the first run.[21]

The Conscious Lovers was performed eight more times during the season of 1722–1723. During the next five years, the Drury Lane company performed the play an average of three times a year. Other theaters did not rush it into production. The company at Goodman's Fields first acted it in January, 1730, and Lincoln's Inn Fields followed in November of that year. Yet afterwards, the play became one of the most popular in the repertoire; it was performed every season until 1775 and many times thereafter. Actors and actresses often chose it for their benefits, a measure of its financial success since they tried to choose profitable plays. Usually it was acted several times a season, as many as fifteen in 1735–1736, thirteen in 1744–1745, and either

[17] B.M. Add. MSS. 34327, f. 6, cited in Rae Blanchard, *The Correspondence of Richard Steele* (Oxford and London, 1941), p. 520, n. 1.

[18] *St. James's Journal*, December 8, 1722.

[19] *Correspondence*, pp. 143–145, n. 2; *St. James's Journal*, November 15, 1722.

[20] John Dennis, *Remarks on a Play, Call'd, The Conscious Lovers, A Comedy*, in *Critical Works*, II, 274.

[21] For a detailed discussion of the controversy, see Loftis, pp. 195–213.

twelve or thirteen as late as 1759–1760.[22] It reached its greatest popularity as measured by the number of performances in the 1730's and 1740's. A table of performances for five decades excluding the initial season indicates its rise and gradual decline on stage:

1723–33	41 performances
1733–43	85 performances
1743–53	86 performances
1753–63	68 performances
1763–73	36 performances[23]

Although performances began to drop off in the second half of the century, Professor George Winchester Stone shows that *The Conscious Lovers* was the sixth most frequently performed comedy at Drury Lane in the years 1747–1776 and the seventh at Covent Garden.[24] It was often played early in the season, when the management tended to choose old favorites, and it continued to be chosen for benefits. As charity benefits became popular, the play was often selected as the vehicle for raising money for the relief of poor widows with children, the wards in Middlesex Hospital, or Westminster's new lying-in hospital. With its emphasis on pity and goodness, it must have seemed particularly appropriate for charitable endeavors. The frequency of performances by request of "persons of quality" and by royal command attests its continued respectability.

Only after fifty years did Steele's play finally begin to lose its hold on the English stage. The foreword to Bell's edition in *British Theatre* (1791) suggests the cause for its gradual decline from popularity:

> This play is a very finished production in sentiment and language. If nothing more be needed than a sensible display of virtue to make men happy, good, and wise, we know no comedy that more merits to be at all times popular.
>
> Yet an admirer of the old comedy rises fatigued from this piece as from a tedious lesson. It is as fine as Seneca, as profitable too, but weak humanity requires to be diverted into a sense of duty, and for risibility here is no food.

[22] There is some question about whether it was performed January 14, 1760. See George Winchester Stone, Jr., *The London Stage 1660–1800 Part 4: 1747–1776* (Carbondale, Ill., 1962), II, 768.

[23] *The London Stage 1660–1800 Parts 2, 3, and 4, passim.*

[24] Stone, I, clxiii, clxv.

If this evaluation is an accurate measure, the sententiousness deliberately introduced by Steele but scored by even the earliest critics finally weighed too heavily on audiences. A play could teach a lesson but not a tedious one. For the audiences of the late eighteenth century, *The Conscious Lovers* doubtless proved too dull, too static, and too preachy.

Steele's last comedy was the culmination of his efforts as writer, as moralist, and as reformer, "the last blaze of Sir Richard's glory."[25] He wrote it with the conviction that the theater should serve a social purpose. This belief was apparent in his earliest comedy, *The Funeral* (1701), as the epilogue suggests:

> The Stage to Wisdom's no Fantastick Way,
> Athens her self learn't Virtue at a Play.

To impart virtue Steele replaced the *double-entendre* and innuendo of Restoration dialogue with the utmost decency and decorum. He relegated the lively lovers to the subplot and promoted the more serious pair. This was a reversal of the pattern of such Restoration comedies as *The Country Wife* and *The Man of Mode*, in which more or less serious young lovers provide subplots. In *The Funeral* Sharlot and Lord Hardy, like Etherege's Emilia and Young Bellair, are slightly ludicrous, not altogether admirable. Steele made his young lovers excessively shy; they splutter, blush, and endure awkward pauses when they meet. In the end, however, they are embarrassingly vocal, and in blank verse.

In *The Lying Lover* (1703), Steele went further toward moralizing comedy, turning the fifth act into a maudlin condemnation of dueling. When this play was "damn'd for its Piety,"[26] he reverted to laughing comedy in *The Tender Husband* (1705). The titular plot concerns the reformation of a fashionable wife, but only three scenes touch it, and only one (V.i) can be considered sentimental. Unlike its Restoration antecedents, however, this unsentimental comedy is free of sexual promiscuity. Oddly enough, *The Tender Husband*, although very funny, was not unusually popular; it did not surpass *The Funeral* in number of performances. The taste for the sentimental, it would seem, had anticipated Steele's campaign for moral drama.

25 Victor, *Original Letters*, I, 327.

26 *Mr. Steele's Apology for Himself and his Writings*, in *Tracts and Pamphlets by Richard Steele*, ed. Rae Blanchard (Baltimore, 1944), p. 312.

In the *Tatler* in 1709 Steele advocated the stage as a means of encouraging good manners and morals, recommending

> the apt Use of a Theater, as the most agreeable and easie Method of making a Polite and Moral Gentry, which would end in rendring the rest of the People regular in their Behaviour, and ambitious of laudable Undertakings.[27]

In the *Spectator* he continued to urge drama which would promote moral and social improvement. Finally, in *The Conscious Lovers* he embodied his fully developed dramatic theory. His stated intention was to create "an innocent performance," by which to instruct his audience through "the effect of example and precept."[28] He created moral characters to illustrate their virtues through actions (example) and instructive dialogue (precept). Since paragons and preaching have little connection with traditional theories of comedy, he redefined comic drama: ". . . anything that has its foundation in happiness and success must be allowed to be the object of comedy, and sure it must be an improvement of it to introduce a joy too exquisite for laughter, that can have no spring but in delight. . . ."[29] Tears springing from "reason and good sense" became, then, proper responses.

Steele found justification for his theory of comedy in Terence, who was widely considered superior to all others in the purity of his language.[30] Steele was less interested, however, in Terence's style than in his sedateness, his sententious tone, and his moral characters. In 1712 he had discussed Terence's sententiousness in *Spectator* No. 502. The paper is a critique of the *Self-Tormentor* in which Steele commends the "worthy Sentiments" and continues:

> It is from the Beginning to the End a perfect Picture of humane Life, but I did not observe in the Whole one Passage that could raise a Laugh. How well disposed must that People be, who could be entertained with Satisfaction by so sober and polite Mirth!

[27] *Tatler*, No. 8. [28] The Preface, ll. 14–16.
[29] *Ibid.*, ll. 26–30.
[30] Many critics of the time felt his plots and characterizations matched the excellence of his style. See, for example, Charles Gildon's "Letter to Mr. D'Urfey, Occasioned by his Play, Called the Marriage-Hater Match'd," published with the play (London, 1692). George Colman, in his edition of *The Comedies of Terence, Translated into Familiar Blank Verse*, 2nd ed. (London, 1768), shows the continuity of this appreciation of Terence.

To this he later added the comment that there are "several Incidents which would draw Tears from any Man of Sense, and not one which would move his Laughter."[31] That Steele's reading of Terence was affected by his own sensibility cannot be denied.[32] Although the comedies abound in sententious statements, they are not devoid of laughter, nor was Terence's audience disposed to weep. Steele, having molded his theory of didactic comedy, sought a precedent and found it in Terence, but he read into the plays his personal predilection for the emotional.

Although Steele may have believed that "the whole was writ for the sake of the scene of the fourth act, wherein Mr. Bevil evades the quarrel with his friend,"[33] the precepts also cover the duties of sons, the inhumanity of arranged marriages, the obligations of friendship, the proper behavior of well-bred young men, the dangers of excessive jealousy, and other contemporary topics. Underlying all the moral injunctions is the doctrine of benevolence, the theory that doing good for others brings joy to the heart of the doer, with the corollary notion that weeping for others in their distress is also ennobling and in an odd way pleasurable. Bevil specifically commends the joy of doing good (in II.ii), and the audience experiences the pleasure of weeping with Indiana (in V.iii). Although modern readers may consider Indiana's display of emotion excessive, audiences of Steele's day did not. To them the best scene in the play was V.iii: when Indiana learned the identity of her father, members of the audience wept with her. Characters on stage as well as the audience, then, were expected to demonstrate "the excellence of a right disposition and the natural working of a well-turned spirit."[34]

Steele offered two reasons for choosing his style of comedy. First he contended that laughter, the response produced by ridiculing foolish characters, was an inferior reaction based on scorn, and he preferred to address himself to the goodness of the heart.[35] Second, he argued that Restoration comedy often made disreputable characters, particularly rakes, attractive rather than ridiculous.[36] Bevil was designed by him and accepted by his audience as a repudiation of characters

[31] *Spectator*, No. 521.

[32] For a discussion of eighteenth-century misinterpretations of Terence see Ernest Bernbaum, *The Drama of Sensibility* (Gloucester, Mass., 1958), pp. 11–26.

[33] The Preface, ll. 18–20.

[34] *Ibid.*, ll. 39–40.

[35] Epilogue, *The Lying Lover*.

[36] *Spectator*, No. 75.

like Dorimant, the rakish hero of *The Man of Mode*. Ridicule could still be used "to bring Pretenders and Impostors in Society to a true Light,"[37] but exemplary characters, Steele believed, offered a better means to encourage good morals and manners.

Although Steele could not populate *The Conscious Lovers* entirely with perfect moral specimens, from his point of view the exemplary characters are most significant: Bevil, the fine gentleman; Indiana, the virtuous maiden; Mr. Sealand, the gentlemanly merchant; and Humphrey, the ideal servant. He created models for each class in the audience except the nobility. Bevil and Indiana, who demonstrate "good Manners, good Sense, and common Honesty"[38] which genteel young people should emulate, combat the ill effects of Restoration characters like Dorimant and Harriet. Mr. Sealand offers sharp contrast to the cits of former days. For the upper gallery Humphrey illustrates loyal and dutiful service instead of self-serving trickery.

A second group of characters, who are not exemplary, are ridiculed in the manner of Restoration comedy. Steele again represents three levels of society. Cimberton, the country gentleman of superior lineage, is a "formal, philosophical, pedantic coxcomb."[39] Mrs. Sealand, the social climber, is dissatisfied with her bourgeois status, envious of her daughter's youth and beauty, and vain of her presumed intellectual powers. The servants Tom and Phillis affect the wit and gallantry of their betters, exchanging quips in the style of Dorimants and Harriets. Unlike Mrs. Sealand and Cimberton, they prove amusing rather than contemptible, although the upper-class mannerisms they imitate merit derision.

Myrtle is a variation on a theme in Steele's earlier plays, that of the redeemable delinquent. Although good-hearted and right-thinking, he suffers from excessive jealousy and a hot temper. His reform immediately follows Bevil's proof that he had no cause for jealousy and might have killed unjustly. Cured of his flaws and suitably rewarded, Myrtle murmurs to the last his gratitude to Bevil.

The exemplary and ridiculous characters are designed by Steele at least in part to illustrate social virtues and follies and thereby to improve his audience. The other characters are a by-product of the philosophy of benevolence which makes it reasonable for social flaws to be noticed and easily reformed or, if minor, gently overlooked.

[37] *Tatler*, No. 63.
[38] *Spectator*, No. 65.
[39] II.i. 41–42.

With forgivable faults Steele is convincing. It is his experiment with purely exemplary characters that causes him difficulties. In making Bevil a model of virtue and filial obedience, Steele creates a prig instead of a hero. Young Bevil is a gentleman who has an independent income, an easy temper, and a penchant for reading moral essays. He is blessed with a kindly father and a beautiful, virtuous woman who loves him. His innate virtue destroys the possibility of any internal struggle, and his family and fortune shield him against any struggle with outside forces. It is therefore almost impossible to demonstrate his moral superiority through stage action. Except for his behavior toward Indiana, his only chance to exhibit his virtue is in his refusal to accept Myrtle's challenge (IV.i). For the rest, the audience must depend on speeches about it. As William Hazlitt said, ". . . the whole distinction between virtue and vice . . . is reduced to verbal professions, and a mechanical, infantine goodness."[40] Action is several times delayed while Bevil makes pronouncements on social and moral topics. From the first, if we may believe Steele's critics, audiences squirmed at the tedium of these sermons. Bevil inevitably failed as a hero because of Steele's determination to deal in "example and precept."

Steele was not a profound or consistent moral writer, and consequently Bevil's system of values itself is questionable. Dennis found him "as arrant an Hypocrite as a certain Author"[41] and condemned him for dissembling to his father by pretending to be willing to marry Lucinda. Even Benjamin Victor, Steele's vigorous young defender, saw in the ruse a flaw in Bevil's integrity.[42] What is significant is not that Bevil's view of morality is short-sighted, but rather that Steele, in his attempt to revamp the techniques of comedy for didactic purposes, failed to make virtue pleasing.

For a plot appropriate to his aims Steele turned to the *Andria*. He might have hoped thereby to capitalize upon Terence's reputation, but Dennis and his colleagues criticized the adaptation instead of praising the choice of author. Actually Steele translated speeches no further than I.i, and his play owed little more to Terence than the basic plot outline. In the original an upright young man, trusted by his father, has been betrothed to one girl but is involved with another,

[40] William Hazlitt, *Lectures on the English Comic Writers*, in *The Complete Works of William Hazlitt*, ed. P. P. Howe (London, 1931), VI, 157.

[41] Dennis, *Remarks*, in *Critical Works*, II, 272.

[42] Victor, *Epistle to Sir Richard Steele*, p. 15.

of questionable reputation, who has become pregnant. When the father of the fiancée discovers the illicit relationship, he calls off the match. The young man's father, however, continues mock wedding arrangements in order to test his son. At the suggestion of an eavesdropping servant, the hero pretends compliance, knowing it will not lead to marriage, but in so doing he infuriates his friend who really loves the supposed bride and therefore feels misused. All works out happily when a traveler arrives and reveals that the girl, now delivered of her child, is the long-lost daughter of the prospective father-in-law. Neither of the women appears on stage; the pathos of the situation is never exploited. The tone is somewhat serious, although the young servant's machinations are comic.

To Terence's outline of plot and character, Steele added the five female characters, Cimberton, Myrtle's disguise scenes, and Tom's romance. He also anglicized and modernized characters. The *Andria* had two fathers, but it was Steele who made one a knight and the other a merchant. Terence had an unwed mother; Steele substituted an unfortunate virgin.

The plot structure is similar to that of *The Funeral*, with a serious main plot, a comic subplot, and an echoing of the love motif in the ridiculous romance of the young servants. The Indiana-Bevil plot line rests on the difficulty of convincing Sir John, who seeks an advantageous match for his son, of the suitability of a young incognita. To make the action more sedate, Steele departs from the *Andria* by choosing the faithful old retainer Humphrey rather than young Tom as manipulator. He does not introduce a returning traveler to resolve the difficulties, as had Terence, but his denouement nevertheless suffers from improbability: Indiana fortuitously discovers her long-lost father in Sealand, who has inexplicably changed his name, lost contact with his native Bristol, and thus proved impossible to find. The reunion is made more dramatic and less probable by Isabella's very unlikely decision not to identify herself to her brother and her remarkable ability to hold her tongue.

In the *Andria* the love of the friend for the fiancée is quite insignificant, scantily developed, and only casually touched in the denouement. Steele greatly enlarges the subplot and gives it the humor lacking in his main plot. In the attempts of Myrtle to prevent Lucinda's marriage to Cimberton, Steele merges laughing comedy with the sentimental. Basically Lucinda is an obedient daughter and Myrtle an honorable young man, both cast in the sentimental fashion;

yet the two, like Campley and Harriet in *The Funeral*, have far more liveliness than can be contained in exemplary characters. Myrtle disguises himself as the lawyer Bramble and again as old Sir Geoffry Cimberton, and both times he succeeds in fooling Mrs. Sealand and Cimberton, but he does not then introduce a false contract or elope with Lucinda as earlier deceivers would have done. The disguise scenes are reminiscent of Restoration comedy, but they prove to be mere vestiges of the earlier mode, for when the tradition of disguise and dupery strikes against Steele's ethical code, the characters are rendered incapable of seizing the advantages gained by their trickery. The disguise scenes provide welcome sight comedy, but they do not ultimately affect the outcome of the plot.

As in *The Funeral* and many earlier comedies, the amours of the servants provide a humorous counterpoint to the other love affairs. Tom and Phillis talk of the opera, as do Bevil and Indiana, and there is a serenade. They disguise their true feelings for one another. They exchange pretty remarks and witty compliments. They too must be concerned about the financial aspects of marriage. All in all, their emulation of the upper class produces a satirical effect surprising in the context of Bevil's solemnity. Although Steele believed in exemplary characters, his talent lay in creating comic ones. If audiences wept for Indiana, they widely applauded Tom and Phillis.

The Conscious Lovers, then, is a fusion of Restoration conventions of characterization and plot with Steele's own dramatic concepts rather than a totally new kind of comedy. Steele gathers exemplary characters, sententious dialogue, and serious, high-minded action into the main plot line. Most of the preceptual speeches and all the exemplary characters are connected with it. Terence's seriousness is preserved, even intensified, and an emotional climax turns moral sentiment to feeling. The Restoration mode, stripped of impropriety, shapes the subplot. Lucinda is spirited, Myrtle resorts to disguises, the young servants act as go-betweens and suggest or support light-hearted schemes. Mrs. Sealand and Cimberton are pretentious, absurd, and easily gulled. But Restoration comedy, when chastened by Steele, loses its bite. Although the kind of dialogue associated with the humours characters is retained, the repartee of the gay couple is virtually lost; only Tom and Phillis now display any tartness in conversation. The tone of the dialogue becomes humorous rather than witty; the trickery brings no results; the absurd characters are not suitably punished for their folly. Nevertheless, the subplot produces laughter, which, as Colley Cibber knew, was required by an English audience.[43]

Steele divided his serious and comic materials more pointedly than earlier writers, but he was certainly not the first to have a serious plot or commendable characters. Yet it is *The Conscious Lovers* that is recognized as the first thoroughly sentimental English comedy, and it unquestionably had a profound effect on stage history. Why? First of all, Steele's timing was right. Theatergoers were ready for a change, as they had indicated by their lack of enthusiasm for *The Tender Husband*. In such periodicals as the *Tatler* and *Spectator* they were primed for moral comedy. In his last play Steele was able to crystallize the feelings and intellectual tendencies of his time in dramatic form. He introduced issues important to his audience, for example, the crumbling of class barriers, the evils of arranged marriages, dueling. Most important, he brought to the stage sentimental, lusciously emotional scenes which perfectly suited the English sensibility.

Secondly, Steele himself made an issue of the theory of comedy. Earlier writers had quietly introduced sentimental touches, but Steele wrote a play to demonstrate his theory and accurately described the theory in the preface. *The Conscious Lovers* was an open challenge to the audience's taste for Restoration comedies and a call to playwrights for a new approach. In his dedication to the King he envisioned the play as "the prelude of what, by your Majesty's influence and favor, may be attempted in future representations." Most critics rejected his theory, and on reasonable grounds. Yet audiences warmed to it, becoming even more appreciative in the 1730's and 1740's when sentimentalism was growing stronger.

The play had as great a literary impact as Steele could have wished. James J. Lynch called it "probably the most significant contribution of the age to drama" in terms of influencing later plays and inspiring imitations.[44] Most widely imitated were the moral tone, pathetic heroine, serious and improbable main plot, on-stage reformation, and good-natured characters; the exemplary hero and sententiousness, or "example and precept," proved less durable. The theater became moral, as Steele would have it, but also lifeless and unoriginal. Pathetic heroines rescued from their despair by improbable discoveries became standard. Voltaire said that his Zaïre, recognized by the cross she wore, was suggested by Indiana and her bracelet. Edward Moore's Fidelia in *The Foundling* (1748) and Richard

[43] Theophilus Cibber, *Lives of the Poets* IV, 120.

[44] *Box Pit and Gallery* (Berkeley and Los Angeles, 1953), p. 39.

Cumberland's Augusta in *The Fashionable Lover* (1772) are two of the many English imitations of Indiana. The interest the plays lost in comic trickery and disguise was replaced by intricate, improbable, and finally melodramatic plots. If exemplary heroes proved boring, reformed rakes were warmly accepted. But probably the most telling change in English comedy of the eighteenth century was the good nature represented in the characters and expected of the audience. For it was to this bent in English character that Steele and later playwrights appealed.

As might be expected, when Goldsmith and Sheridan attempted to return to laughing comedy in the late 1760's and 1770's, they created something quite different from the Restoration plays, and the difference can be traced to the trends popularized by Steele. Despite their mockery of false benevolence, it is still benevolence that is the chief virtue, as Young Honeywood's last speech and Charles Surface's behavior to Stanley demonstrate. The romance of Leontine and Olivia in *The Good Natur'd Man* closely resembles that of Bevil and Indiana. In *The School for Scandal* Maria is as chaste as Indiana if less emotional, and she displays no more liveliness or gaiety. In *The Rivals* the serious love of Julia and Faulkland has been relegated again to the subplot, but it is treated sentimentally; she is virtuous, he repentant. With few exceptions characters in Goldsmith's and Sheridan's plays are either demonstrably honorable, readily repentant, pleasantly eccentric, or recognizably villainous. The morality is that of Steele, but now it is wrong to talk about it. Goldsmith and Sheridan changed the emphasis on the values of Steele and other sentimental writers, but they did not discard them, any more than Steele had discarded the techniques of Restoration comedy.

If the influence of Steele can be seen in these playwrights, it is far more evident in the Cumberlands and Kellys that produced most later eighteenth-century drama. Steele, to the detriment of the English stage, accomplished the reforms he sought.

SHIRLEY STRUM KENNY

The Catholic University of America

THE CONSCIOUS LOVERS

Illud genus narrationis, quod in personis positum est, debet habere sermonis festivitatem, animorum dissimilitudinem, gravitatem, lenitatem, spem, metum, suspicionem, desiderium, dissimulationem, misericordiam, rerum varietates, fortunae commutationem, insperatum incommodum, subitam letitiam, jucundum exitum rerum.

Cicero, *Rhetorica ad Herennium*, I.viii.

The kind of narration based on characters ought to have pleasantry of discourse, diversity of spirits, gravity, gentleness, hope, fear, suspicion, desire, hypocrisy, compassion, variety of occurrences, changes of fortune, unexpected misfortune, sudden joy, and a happy ending.

This work is no longer attributed to Cicero.

To the King

May it please your Majesty,

After having aspired to the highest and most laudable ambition, that of following the cause of liberty, I should not have humbly petitioned your Majesty for a direction of the theater had I not believed success in that province an happiness much to be wished by an honest man and highly conducing to the prosperity of the Commonwealth. It is in this view I lay before your Majesty a comedy, which the audience, in justice to themselves, has supported and encouraged, and is the prelude of what, by your Majesty's influence and favor, may be attempted in future representations. 5 10

The imperial mantle, the royal vestment, and the shining diadem are what strike ordinary minds; but your Majesty's native goodness, your passion for justice and her constant assessor mercy is what continually surrounds you, in the view of intelligent spirits, and gives hope to the suppliant, who sees he has more than succeeded in giving Your Majesty an opportunity of doing good. Our King is above the greatness of royalty, and every act of his will which makes another man happy has ten times more charms in it than one that makes himself appear raised above the condition of others. But even this carries unhappiness with it; for calm dominion, equal grandeur, and familiar greatness do not easily affect the imagination of the vulgar, who cannot see power but in terror; and as fear moves mean spirits and love prompts great ones to obey, the insinuations of malcontents are directed accordingly, and the unhappy people are ensnared, from want of reflection, into disrespectful ideas of their gracious and amiable Sovereign, and then only begin to apprehend the greatness of their master when they have incurred his displeasure. 15 20 25 30

As your Majesty was invited to the throne of a willing people for their own sakes and has ever enjoyed it with contempt

---

the King] George I.

4–5. *a direction . . . theater*] The King appointed Steele governor of Drury Lane Theatre in 1714.

23. *equal*] tranquil. 23. *familiar*] affable.

of the ostentation of it, we beseech you to protect us who revere your title as we love your person. 'Tis to be a savage to be a rebel, and they who have fallen from you have not so much forfeited their allegiance as lost their humanity. And therefore, if it were only to preserve myself from the imputation of being amongst the insensible and abandoned, I would beg permission in the most public manner possible to profess myself, with the utmost sincerity and zeal,

SIRE,

Your MAJESTY'S

Most Devoted Subject and Servant,

RICHARD STEELE

The Preface

This comedy has been received with universal acceptance, for it was in every part excellently performed; and there needs no other applause of the actors but that they excelled according to the dignity and difficulty of the character they represented. But this great favor done to the work in acting renders the expectation still the greater from the author to keep up the spirit in the representation of the closet or any other circumstance of the reader, whether alone or in company. To which I can only say that it must be remembered a play is to be seen and is made to be represented with the advantage of action nor can appear but with half the spirit without it; for the greatest effect of a play in reading is to excite the reader to go see it; and when he does so, it is then a play has the effect of example and precept. 5 10

The chief design of this was to be an innocent performance, and the audience have abundantly showed how ready they are to support what is visibly intended that way; nor do I make any difficulty to acknowledge that the whole was writ for the sake of the scene of the fourth act, wherein Mr. Bevil evades the quarrel with his friend, and hope it may have some effect upon the Goths and Vandals that frequent the theaters, or a more polite audience may supply their absence. 15 20

But this incident and the case of the father and daughter are esteemed by some people no subjects of comedy; but I cannot be of their mind, for anything that has its foundation in happiness and success must be allowed to be the object of comedy, and sure it must be an improvement of it to introduce a joy too exquisite for laughter, that can have no spring but in delight, which is the case of this young lady. I must therefore contend that the tears which were shed on that occasion flowed from reason and good sense and that men ought not to be laughed at for weeping till we are come to a more clear notion of what is to be imputed to the hardness of the head and the softness of the heart; and I think it was 25 30 35

7. *closet*] small, private room; study.

very politely said of Mr. Wilks to one who told him there was a general weeping for Indiana, "I'll warrant he'll fight ne'er the worse for that." To be apt to give way to the impressions of humanity is the excellence of a right disposition and the natural working of a well-turned spirit. But as I have suffered by critics who are got no farther than to inquire whether they ought to be pleased or not, I would willingly find them properer matter for their employment, and revive here a song which was omitted for want of a performer and designed for the entertainment of Indiana; Signor Carbonelli instead of it played on the fiddle, and it is for want of a singer that such advantageous things are said of an instrument which were designed for a voice. The song is the distress of a love-sick maid and may be a fit entertainment for some small critics to examine whether the passion is just or the distress male or female. 40 45 50

I

From place to place forlorn I go,
With downcast eyes, a silent shade;
Forbidden to declare my woe;
To speak, till spoken to, afraid. 55

II

My inward pangs, my secret grief,
My soft consenting looks betray:
He loves, but gives me no relief:
Why speaks not he who may?

It remains to say a word concerning Terence, and I am extremely surprised to find what Mr. Cibber told me prove a 60

61. me] *O1–2, D1*; *om. O3.*

---

36. *Mr. Wilks*] Robert Wilks, one of the actor-managers of Drury Lane, played Myrtle.

37. *general*] The Honorable Brigadier General Charles Churchill, whose mistress Anne Oldfield played the role.

45. *Signor Carbonelli*] a virtuoso violinist who had recently come from Italy.

52–59. An earlier version entitled "The Love-sick Maid" appeared in *The Theatre*, No. 18.

61. *Mr. Cibber*] Colley Cibber, one of the actor-managers of Drury Lane.

truth, that what I valued myself so much upon, the translation of him, should be imputed to me as a reproach. Mr. Cibber's zeal for the work, his care and application in instructing the actors and altering the disposition of the scenes 65 when I was, through sickness, unable to cultivate such things myself, has been a very obliging favor and friendship to me. For this reason, I was very hardly persuaded to throw away Terence's celebrated funeral and take only the bare authority of the young man's character, and how I have worked 70 it into an Englishman and made use of the same circumstances of discovering a daughter when we least hoped for one is humbly submitted to the learned reader.

62–63. *the translation of him*] the adaptation of Terence's *Andria.*
69. *Terence's celebrated funeral*] a scene in the *Andria.*
70. *the young man's character*] Pamphilus in the *Andria.*
72. *discovering a daughter*] See Introduction, pp. xxi–xxii.

PROLOGUE

By Mr. Welsted
Spoken by Mr. Wilks

To win your hearts, and to secure your praise,
The comic-writers strive by various ways:
By subtle stratagems they act their game,
And leave untried no avenue to fame.
One writes the spouse a beating from his wife; 5
And says, "Each stroke was copied from the life."
Some fix all wit and humor in grimace,
And make a livelihood of Pinkey's face.
Here one gay show and costly habits tries,
Confiding to the judgment of your eyes. 10
Another smuts his scene, a cunning shaver,
Sure of the rakes' and of the wenches' favor.
Oft have these arts prevailed; and one may guess,
If practiced o'er again, would find success.
But the bold sage, the poet of tonight, 15
By new and desp'rate rules resolved to write;
Fain would he give more just applauses rise,
And please by wit that scorns the aids of vice;
The praise he seeks, from worthier motives springs,
Such praise as praise to those that give it brings. 20
Your aid, most humbly sought, then, Britons, lend,
And lib'ral mirth like lib'ral men defend:
No more let ribaldry, with license writ,
Usurp the name of eloquence or wit;
No more let lawless farce uncensured go, 25
The lewd dull gleanings of a Smithfield show.
'Tis yours with breeding to refine the age,
To chasten wit, and moralize the stage.
Ye modest, wise and good, ye fair, ye brave,
Tonight the champion of your virtues save, 30
Redeem from long contempt the comic name,
And judge politely for your country's fame.

20. give] *J*; give, *O1–3*, *D1*.

Mr. Welsted] Leonard Welsted, the poet, a friend of Steele.
8. *Pinkey*] William Pinkethman, the comedian.
26. *lewd*] low, vulgar.
26. *a Smithfield show*] one of the "low" amusements of Bartholomew Fair.

DRAMATIS PERSONAE

Men

Sir John Bevil	*Mr. Mills*
Mr. Sealand	*Mr. Williams*
Bevil Junior, in love with Indiana	*Mr. Booth*
Myrtle, in love with Lucinda	*Mr. Wilks*
Cimberton, a coxcomb	*Mr. Griffin*
Humphrey, an old servant to Sir John	*Mr. Shepard*
Tom, servant to Bevil Junior	*Mr. Cibber*
Daniel, a country boy, servant to Indiana	*Mr. Theophilus Cibber*

Women

Mrs. Sealand, second wife to Sealand	*Mrs. Moore*
Isabella, sister to Sealand	*Mrs. Thurmond*
Indiana, Sealand's daughter by his first wife	*Mrs. Oldfield*
Lucinda, Sealand's daughter by his second wife	*Mrs. Booth*
Phillis, maid to Lucinda	*Mrs. Younger*

Scene: *London*

The Conscious Lovers

ACT I

[I.i]

Scene, Sir John Bevil's house. Enter Sir John Bevil *and* Humphrey.

SIR JOHN BEVIL.
Have you ordered that I should not be interrupted while I am dressing?

HUMPHREY.
Yes, sir. I believed you had something of moment to say to me.

SIR JOHN BEVIL.
Let me see, Humphrey; I think it is now full forty years since I first took thee to be about myself. 5

HUMPHREY.
I thank you, sir, it has been an easy forty years, and I have passed 'em without much sickness, care, or labor.

SIR JOHN BEVIL.
Thou hast a brave constitution; you are a year or two older than I am, sirrah. 10

HUMPHREY.
You have ever been of that mind, sir.

SIR JOHN BEVIL.
You knave, you know it; I took thee for thy gravity and sobriety in my wild years.

HUMPHREY.
Ah sir, our manners were formed from our different fortunes, not our different age. Wealth gave a loose to your youth, 15 and poverty put a restraint upon mine.

SIR JOHN BEVIL.
Well, Humphrey, you know I have been a kind master to

---

9. *brave*] excellent.
15. *gave a loose*] freed from restraint.

you; I have used you, for the ingenuous nature I observed in you from the beginning, more like an humble friend than a servant. 20

HUMPHREY.

I humbly beg you'll be so tender of me as to explain your commands, sir, without any farther preparation.

SIR JOHN BEVIL.

I'll tell thee then. In the first place, this wedding of my son's, in all probability—shut the door—will never be at all.

HUMPHREY.

How, sir! Not be at all? For what reason is it carried on in 25 appearance?

SIR JOHN BEVIL.

Honest Humphrey, have patience, and I'll tell thee all in order. I have myself, in some part of my life, lived, indeed, with freedom, but, I hope, without reproach. Now I thought liberty would be as little injurious to my son; therefore, as 30 soon as he grew towards man, I indulged him in living after his own manner. I knew not how, otherwise, to judge of his inclination; for what can be concluded from a behavior under restraint and fear? But what charms me above all expression is that my son has never in the least action, the most 35 distant hint or word, valued himself upon that great estate of his mother's, which, according to our marriage settlement, he has had ever since he came to age.

HUMPHREY.

No, sir; on the contrary, he seems afraid of appearing to enjoy it before you or any belonging to you. He is as dependent 40 and resigned to your will as if he had not a farthing but what must come from your immediate bounty. You have ever acted like a good and generous father, and he like an obedient and grateful son.

SIR JOHN BEVIL.

Nay, his carriage is so easy to all with whom he converses 45 that he is never assuming, never prefers himself to others, nor ever is guilty of that rough sincerity which a man is not called to and certainly disobliges most of his acquaintance.

23–54.] This dialogue, though not an exact translation, closely follows the *Andria*.

To be short, Humphrey, his reputation was so fair in the world that old Sealand, the great India merchant, has offered his only daughter and sole heiress to that vast estate of his as a wife for him. You may be sure I made no difficulties, the match was agreed on, and this very day named for the wedding. 50

HUMPHREY.

What hinders the proceeding? 55

SIR JOHN BEVIL.

Don't interrupt me. You know I was last Thursday at the masquerade; my son, you may remember, soon found us out. He knew his grandfather's habit, which I then wore; and though it was the mode in the last age, yet the maskers, you know, followed us as if we had been the most monstrous figures in that whole assembly. 60

HUMPHREY.

I remember indeed a young man of quality in the habit of a clown that was particularly troublesome.

SIR JOHN BEVIL.

Right. He was too much what he seemed to be. You remember how impertinently he followed, and teased us, and would know who we were. 65

HUMPHREY (*aside*).

I know he has a mind to come into that particular.

SIR JOHN BEVIL.

Ay, he followed us till the gentlemen who led the lady in the Indian mantle presented that gay creature to the rustic and bid him like Cymon in the fable grow polite by falling in love and let that worthy old gentleman alone, meaning me. The clown was not reformed but rudely persisted and offered to force off my mask; with that the gentleman, throwing off his own, appeared to be my son, and in his concern for me tore off that of the nobleman. At this they seized each other, the company called the guards, and in the surprise the lady 70 75

55–93.] Steele changed Terence's funeral to a masquerade.

63. *clown*] bumpkin.

67. *come . . . particular*] i.e., tell me about it.

70. *Cymon*] a dull-witted clod who saw Iphigenia sleeping, fell in love, and consequently began his education in the polite arts. The tale from the *Decameron* (V.i) appears in Dryden's *Fables*.

swooned away, upon which my son quitted his adversary and had now no care but of the lady, when raising her in his arms, "Art thou gone," cried he, "forever? —Forbid it heaven!" She revives at his known voice, and with the most familiar though modest gesture hangs in safety over his shoulder weeping, but wept as in the arms of one before whom she could give herself a loose were she not under observation. While she hides her face in his neck, he carefully conveys her from the company. 80 85

HUMPHREY.

I have observed this accident has dwelt upon you very strongly.

SIR JOHN BEVIL.

Her uncommon air, her noble modesty, the dignity of her person, and the occasion itself drew the whole assembly together; and I soon heard it buzzed about, she was the adopted daughter of a famous sea-officer, who had served in France. Now this unexpected and public discovery of my son's so deep concern for her— 90

HUMPHREY.

Was what I suppose alarmed Mr. Sealand, in behalf of his daughter, to break off the match. 95

SIR JOHN BEVIL.

You are right. He came to me yesterday and said he thought himself disengaged from the bargain, being credibly informed my son was already married, or worse, to the lady at the masquerade. I palliated matters and insisted on our agreement, but we parted with little less than a direct breach between us. 100

HUMPHREY.

Well, sir, and what notice have you taken of all this to my young master?

SIR JOHN BEVIL.

That's what I wanted to debate with you. I have said nothing to him yet. But look you, Humphrey, if there is so much in this amour of his that he denies upon my summons to marry, I have cause enough to be offended; and then by my insisting upon his marrying today, I shall know how far he is 105

96–119.] These speeches parallel Terence.

engaged to this lady in masquerade and from thence only shall be able to take my measures. In the meantime I would have you find out how far that rogue his man is let into his secret. He, I know, will play tricks, as much to cross me as to serve his master. 110

HUMPHREY.

Why do you think so of him, sir? I believe he is no worse than I was for you, at your son's age. 115

SIR JOHN BEVIL.

I see it in the rascal's looks. But I have dwelt on these things too long; I'll go to my son immediately, and while I'm gone, your part is to convince his rogue Tom that I am in earnest. I'll leave him to you.

Exit Sir John Bevil.

HUMPHREY.

Well, though this father and son live as well together as possible, yet their fear of giving each other pain is attended with constant mutual uneasiness. I'm sure I have enough to do to be honest and yet keep well with them both. But they know I love 'em, and that makes the task less painful however. 120 125

Enter Tom, *singing.*

Oh, here's the prince of poor coxcombs, the representative of all the better fed than taught. —Ho! ho! Tom, whither so gay and so airy this morning?

TOM.

Sir, we servants of single gentlemen are another kind of people than you domestic ordinary drudges that do business. We are raised above you. The pleasures of board-wages, tavern-dinners, and many a clear gain—vails, alas, you never heard or dreamt of. 130

HUMPHREY.

Thou hast follies and vices enough for a man of ten thousand a year, though 'tis but as t'other day that I sent for you to town, to put you into Mr. Sealand's family, that you might learn a little before I put you to my young master, who is 135

110. to] *O1–3*; *om. D1.* 117. I'm] *O1, D1*; I am *O2–3.*

131. *board-wages*] wages allowed for servants' food. See *Spectator*, No. 88.
132. *vails*] tips.

too gentle for training such a rude thing as you were into proper obedience. You then pulled off your hat to everyone you met in the street, like a bashful great awkward cub as you were. But your great oaken cudgel when you were a booby became you much better than that dangling stick at your button now you are a fop. That's fit for nothing, except it hangs there to be ready for your master's hand when you are impertinent. 140 145

TOM.

Uncle Humphrey, you know my master scorns to strike his servants. You talk as if the world was now just as it was when my old master and you were in your youth—when you went to dinner because it was so much a clock, when the great blow was given in the hall at the pantry-door, and all the family came out of their holes in such strange dresses and formal faces as you see in the pictures in our long gallery in the country. 150

HUMPHREY.

Why, you wild rogue!

TOM.

You could not fall to your dinner till a formal fellow in a black gown said something over the meat, as if the cook had not made it ready enough. 155

HUMPHREY.

Sirrah, who do you prate after? Despising men of sacred characters! I hope you never heard my good young master talk so like a profligate! 160

TOM.

Sir, I say you put upon me, when I first came to town, about being orderly, and the doctrine of wearing shams to make linen last clean a fortnight, keeping my clothes fresh, and wearing a frock within doors.

HUMPHREY.

Sirrah, I gave you those lessons because I supposed at that 165

151. came] *O1–2, D1*; come *O3*.

138. *rude*] unpolished, inexperienced.

141. *oaken cudgel*] the unfashionable walking stick used by laborers.

142–143. *that . . . button*] a walking stick attached to his coat button, a style affected by fashionable servants.

162. *shams*] false shirt-fronts.

164. *frock*] a loose coat worn by a worker to keep his clothes clean.

time your master and you might have dined at home every day and cost you nothing; then you might have made a good family servant. But the gang you have frequented since at chocolate-houses and taverns in a continual round of noise and extravagance— 170

TOM.

I don't know what you heavy inmates call noise and extravagance, but we gentlemen who are well fed and cut a figure, sir, think it a fine life, and that we must be very pretty fellows who are kept only to be looked at.

HUMPHREY.

Very well, sir. I hope the fashion of being lewd and extravagant, despising of decency and order, is almost at an end, since it is arrived at persons of your quality. 175

TOM.

Master Humphrey, ha! ha! you were an unhappy lad to be sent up to town in such queer days as you were. Why now, sir, the lackeys are the men of pleasure of the age, the top-gamesters and many a laced coat about town have had their education in our parti-colored regiment. We are false lovers, have a taste of music, poetry, billet-doux, dress, politics, ruin damsels, and when we are weary of this lewd town and have a mind to take up, whip into our masters' wigs and linen and marry fortunes. 180 185

HUMPHREY.

Hey-day!

TOM.

Nay, sir, our order is carried up to the highest dignities and distinctions; step but into the Painted Chamber, and by our titles you'd take us all for men of quality. Then again, come down to the Court of Requests, and you see us all laying our broken heads together for the good of the nation. And though 190

---

181. *many . . . coat*] many gentlemen.

182. *in . . . regiment*] i.e., as menservants.

185. *take up*] mend our ways.

189. *the Painted Chamber*] a room in the House of Parliament where servants of members waited for their patrons. While there, they referred to each other by the names of their masters.

191. *the Court of Requests*] the ancient building in which the House of Lords met. Here servants talked politics, sometimes coming to blows.

we never carry a question *nemine contradicente*, yet this I can say with a safe conscience—and I wish every gentleman of our cloth could lay his hand upon his heart and say the same —that I never took so much as a single mug of beer for my vote in all my life. 195

HUMPHREY.

Sirrah, there is no enduring your extravagance; I'll hear you prate no longer. I wanted to see you to inquire how things go with your master, as far as you understand them; I suppose he knows he is to be married today. 200

TOM.

Ay, sir, he knows it and is dressed as gay as the sun; but, between you and I, my dear, he has a very heavy heart under all that gaiety. As soon as he was dressed, I retired, but overheard him sigh in the most heavy manner. He walked thoughtfully to and fro in the room, then went into his closet; when he came out, he gave me this for his mistress, whose maid you know— 205

HUMPHREY.

Is passionately fond of your fine person.

TOM.

The poor fool is so tender, and loves to hear me talk of the world, and the plays, operas, and ridottos for the winter; the parks and Belsize for our summer diversions; and "Lard!" says she, "You are so wild—but you have a world of humor—" 210

HUMPHREY.

Coxcomb! Well, but why don't you run with your master's letter to Mrs. Lucinda, as he ordered you? 215

198. there is] *O1, D1*; there's *O2–3*. 202. Ay] *O1, D1*; *om. O2–3.*

---

193. *nemine contradicente*] unanimously.

194–195. *of our cloth*] of our profession.

211. *ridottos*] a new kind of musical entertainment introduced at the Opera House in the Haymarket in 1722, the year *The Conscious Lovers* was produced.

212. *Belsize*] an estate less than two miles from London used for public entertainments in the summer. Its gardens, refreshments, and amusements predated those of Vauxhall and Ranelagh.

216. *Mrs.*] an abbreviation for "mistress," a term used for any adult woman whether married or not.

TOM.

Because Mrs. Lucinda is not so easily come at as you think for.

HUMPHREY.

Not easily come at? Why sirrah, are not her father and my old master agreed that she and Mr. Bevil are to be one flesh 220 before tomorrow morning?

TOM.

It's no matter for that; her mother, it seems, Mrs. Sealand, has not agreed to it, and you must know, Mr. Humphrey, that in that family the gray mare is the better horse.

HUMPHREY.

What dost thou mean? 225

TOM.

In one word, Mrs. Sealand pretends to have a will of her own and has provided a relation of hers, a stiff, starched philosopher and a wise fool, for her daughter; for which reason, for these ten past days, she has suffered no message nor letter from my master to come near her. 230

HUMPHREY.

And where had you this intelligence?

TOM.

From a foolish fond soul, that can keep nothing from me—one that will deliver this letter too, if she is rightly managed.

HUMPHREY.

What? Her pretty handmaid, Mrs. Phillis?

TOM.

Even she, sir; this is the very hour, you know, she usually 235 comes hither, under a pretense of a visit to your housekeeper forsooth, but in reality to have a glance at—

HUMPHREY.

Your sweet face, I warrant you.

TOM.

Nothing else in nature; you must know, I love to fret and play with the little wanton— 240

HUMPHREY.

Play with the little wanton! What will this world come to?

TOM.

I met her this morning in a new manteau and petticoat, not

---

242. *manteau and petticoat*] a gown open in front, displaying an underskirt.

a bit the worse for her lady's wearing, and she has always new thoughts and new airs with new clothes. Then she never fails to steal some glance or gesture from every visitant 245 at their house, and is indeed the whole town of coquettes at second hand. But here she comes; in one motion she speaks and describes herself better than all the words in the world can.

HUMPHREY.

Then I hope, dear sir, when your own affair is over, you will 250 be so good as to mind your master's with her.

TOM.

Dear Humphrey, you know my master is my friend, and those are people I never forget.

HUMPHREY.

Sauciness itself! But I'll leave you to do your best for him.

Exit.

Enter Phillis.

PHILLIS.

Oh, Mr. Thomas, is Mrs. Sugar-key at home? Lard, one is 255 almost ashamed to pass along the streets. The town is quite empty and nobody of fashion left in it; and the ordinary people do so stare to see anything—dressed like a woman of condition—as it were on the same floor with them pass by. Alas! Alas! It is a sad thing to walk! Oh Fortune! Fortune! 260

TOM.

What? A sad thing to walk? Why, Madame Phillis, do you wish yourself lame?

PHILLIS.

No, Mr. Tom, but I wish I were generally carried in a coach or chair, and of a fortune neither to stand nor go, but to totter, or slide, to be short-sighted, or stare, to fleer in the face, 265 to look distant, to observe, to overlook, yet all become me; and, if I was rich, I could twire and loll as well as the best of them. Oh Tom! Tom! Is it not a pity that you should be so great a coxcomb and I so great a coquette and yet be such poor devils as we are? 270

TOM.

Mrs. Phillis, I am your humble servant for that—

---

265. *fleer*] laugh or smile scornfully.
267. *twire*] give covert glances.

PHILLIS.

Yes, Mr. Thomas, I know how much you are my humble servant, and know what you said to Mrs. Judy, upon seeing her in one of her lady's cast manteaus; that anyone would have thought her the lady, and that she had ordered the other 275 to wear it till it sat easy, for now only it was becoming; to my lady it was only a covering, to Mrs. Judy it was a habit. This you said, after somebody or other. Oh, Tom! Tom! Thou art as false and as base as the best gentleman of them all; but, you wretch, talk to me no more on the old odious 280 subject. Don't, I say.

TOM (*in a submissive tone, retiring*).

I know not how to resist your commands, madam.

PHILLIS.

Commands about parting are grown mighty easy to you of late.

TOM (*aside*).

Oh, I have her; I have nettled and put her into the right 285 temper to be wrought upon, and set a-prating. —Why truly, to be plain with you, Mrs. Phillis, I can take little comfort of late in frequenting your house.

PHILLIS.

Pray, Mr. Thomas, what is it all of a sudden offends your nicety at our house? 290

TOM.

I don't care to speak particulars, but I dislike the whole.

PHILLIS.

I thank you, sir, I am a part of that whole.

TOM.

Mistake me not, good Phillis.

PHILLIS.

Good Phillis! Saucy enough. But however—

TOM.

I say, it is that thou art a part which gives me pain for the 295 disposition of the whole. You must know, madam, to be serious, I am a man, at the bottom, of prodigious nice honor. You are too much exposed to company at your house. To be

292. a] *O1, D1*; *om. O2–3.*

274. *cast*] discarded.

plain, I don't like so many that would be your mistress's lovers whispering to you. 300

PHILLIS.

Don't think to put that upon me. You say this because I wrung you to the heart when I touched your guilty conscience about Judy.

TOM.

Ah Phillis! Phillis! If you but knew my heart!

PHILLIS.

I know too much on't. 305

TOM.

Nay then, poor Crispo's fate and mine are one. Therefore give me leave to say, or sing at least, as he does upon the same occasion—

Sings "Se vedete," &c.

PHILLIS.

What, do you think I'm to be fobbed off with a song? I don't question but you have sung the same to Mrs. Judy too. 310

TOM.

Don't disparage your charms, good Phillis, with jealousy of so worthless an object; besides, she is a poor hussy, and if you doubt the sincerity of my love, you will allow me true to my interest. You are a fortune, Phillis—

PHILLIS [*aside*].

What would the fop be at now? —In good time, indeed, you 315 shall be setting up for a fortune!

TOM.

Dear Mrs. Phillis, you have such a spirit that we shall never be dull in marriage when we come together. But I tell you, you are a fortune, and you have an estate in my hands.

He pulls out a purse; she eyes it.

PHILLIS.

What pretense have I to what is in your hands, Mr. Tom? 320

---

306. *Crispo*] This hero of an Italian opera is falsely accused of deceit and sings "*Se vedete*": "If you see/ My Thoughts/ Ye just Gods, defend/ The Innocence of my Heart./ No one hears me,/ And you are silent:/ Wicked Malice/ Condemns me, and/ Deceives my Father" (translation from the English edition printed by Thomas Wood, 1721).

309. *fobbed off*] cajoled.

316. *setting up for*] trying to get.

TOM.

As thus: there are hours, you know, when a lady is neither pleased or displeased, neither sick or well, when she lolls or loiters, when she's without desires from having more of everything than she knows what to do with.

PHILLIS.

Well, what then? 325

TOM.

When she has not life enough to keep her bright eyes quite open to look at her own dear image in the glass.

PHILLIS.

Explain thyself, and don't be so fond of thy own prating.

TOM.

There are also prosperous and good-natured moments, as when a knot or a patch is happily fixed, when the complex- 330 ion particularly flourishes.

PHILLIS.

Well, what then? I have not patience!

TOM.

Why then, or on the like occasions, we servants who have skill to know how to time business, see when such a pretty folded thing as this (*shows a letter*) may be presented, laid, or 335 dropped, as best suits the present humor. And, madam, because it is a long wearisome journey to run through all the several stages of a lady's temper, my master, who is the most reasonable man in the world, presents you this to bear your charges on the road. *Gives her the purse.* 340

PHILLIS.

Now you think me a corrupt hussy.

TOM.

Oh fie, I only think you'll take the letter.

PHILLIS.

Nay, I know you do, but I know my own innocence; I take it for my mistress's sake.

TOM.

I know it, my pretty one, I know it. 345

---

330. *knot*] ribbon bow to decorate a gown.
330. *patch*] beauty spot.

PHILLIS.

Yes, I say I do it, because I would not have my mistress deluded by one who gives no proof of his passion; but I'll talk more of this, as you see me on my way home. No, Tom, I assure thee, I take this trash of thy master's, not for the value of the thing but as it convinces me he has a true respect for 350 my mistress. I remember a verse to the purpose:

They may be false who languish and complain,
But they who part with money never feign. *Exeunt.*

[I.ii] *Bevil Junior's lodgings.* Bevil Junior, *reading.*

BEVIL JUNIOR.

These moral writers practice virtue after death. This charming Vision of Mirza! Such an author consulted in a morning sets the spirit for the vicissitudes of the day better than the glass does a man's person. But what a day have I to go through! To put on an easy look with an aching heart—if 5 this lady my father urges me to marry should not refuse me, my dilemma is insupportable. But why should I fear it? Is not she in equal distress with me? Has not the letter I have sent her this morning confessed my inclination to another? Nay, have I not moral assurances of her engagements too to 10 my friend Myrtle? It's impossible but she must give in to it, for, sure, to be denied is a favor any man may pretend to. It must be so. Well then, with the assurance of being rejected, I think I may confidently say to my father I am ready to marry her. Then let me resolve upon what I am not very 15 good at, though it is an honest dissimulation.

Enter Tom.

TOM.

Sir John Bevil, sir, is in the next room.

BEVIL JUNIOR.

Dunce! Why did not you bring him in?

---

1. *after death*] Addison had died in 1719.
2. *Vision of Mirza*] a philosophical oriental tale by Addison which appears in the *Spectator* No. 159.
4. *glass*] mirror.

TOM.

I told him, sir, you were in your closet.

BEVIL JUNIOR.

I thought you had known, sir, it was my duty to see my father anywhere. 20 *Going himself to the door.*

TOM (*aside*).

The Devil's in my master! He has always more wit than I have.

Bevil Junior *introducing* Sir John Bevil.

BEVIL JUNIOR.

Sir, you are the most gallant, the most complaisant of all parents. Sure 'tis not a compliment to say these lodgings are 25 yours. Why would you not walk in, sir?

SIR JOHN BEVIL.

I was loath to interrupt you unseasonably on your wedding day.

BEVIL JUNIOR.

One to whom I am beholden for my birthday might have used less ceremony. 30

SIR JOHN BEVIL.

Well, son, I have intelligence you have writ to your mistress this morning. It would please my curiosity to know the contents of a wedding-day letter, for courtship must then be over.

BEVIL JUNIOR.

I assure you, sir, there was no insolence in it upon the prospect of such a vast fortune's being added to our family but 35 much acknowledgment of the lady's greater desert.

SIR JOHN BEVIL.

But, dear Jack, are you in earnest in all this? And will you really marry her?

BEVIL JUNIOR.

Did I ever disobey any command of yours, sir? Nay, any inclination that I saw you bent upon? 40

SIR JOHN BEVIL.

Why, I can't say you have, son; but methinks in this whole

37. greater] *O1–2, D1*; great *O3.*

23.1. *introducing*] bringing in.

business you have not been so warm as I could have wished you. You have visited her, it's true, but you have not been particular. Everyone knows you can say and do as handsome things as any man, but you have done nothing but lived in the general, been complaisant only. 45

BEVIL JUNIOR.
As I am ever prepared to marry if you bid me, so I am ready to let it alone if you will have me.

Humphrey *enters unobserved.*

SIR JOHN BEVIL.
Look you there now! Why, what am I to think of this so absolute and so indifferent a resignation? 50

BEVIL JUNIOR.
Think? That I am still your son, sir. Sir, you have been married, and I have not. And you have, sir, found the inconvenience there is when a man weds with too much love in his head. I have been told, sir, that at the time you married, you made a mighty bustle on the occasion. There was challenging and fighting, scaling walls, locking up the lady, and the gallant under an arrest for fear of killing all his rivals. Now, sir, I suppose you having found the ill consequences of these strong passions and prejudices in preference of one woman to another in case of a man's becoming a widower— 55 60

SIR JOHN BEVIL.
How is this?

BEVIL JUNIOR.
I say, sir, experience has made you wiser in your care of me. For, sir, since you lost my dear mother, your time has been so heavy, so lonely, and so tasteless that you are so good as to guard me against the like unhappiness by marrying me prudentially by way of bargain and sale. For, as you well judge, a woman that is espoused for a fortune is yet a better bargain if she dies; for then a man still enjoys what he did marry, the money, and is disencumbered of what he did not marry, the woman. 65 70

55. have] *O1–3*; have have *D1.*

45. *particular*] especially attentive.

SIR JOHN BEVIL.

But pray, sir, do you think Lucinda then a woman of such little merit?

BEVIL JUNIOR.

Pardon me, sir, I don't carry it so far neither; I am rather afraid I shall like her too well; she has, for one of her fortune, 75
a great many needless and superfluous good qualities.

SIR JOHN BEVIL.

I am afraid, son, there's something I don't see yet, something that's smothered under all this raillery.

BEVIL JUNIOR.

Not in the least, sir. If the lady is dressed and ready, you see I am. I suppose the lawyers are ready too. 80

HUMPHREY (*aside*).

This may grow warm, if I don't interpose. —Sir, Mr. Sealand is at the coffeehouse and has sent to speak with you.

SIR JOHN BEVIL.

Oh! That's well! Then I warrant the lawyers are ready. Son, you'll be in the way, you say—

BEVIL JUNIOR.

If you please, sir, I'll take a chair and go to Mr. Sealand's, 85
where the young lady and I will wait your leisure.

SIR JOHN BEVIL.

By no means. The old fellow will be so vain if he sees—

BEVIL JUNIOR.

Ay, but the young lady, sir, will think me so indifferent—

HUMPHREY (*aside to* Bevil Junior).

Ay, there you are right. Press your readiness to go to the bride—he won't let you. 90

BEVIL JUNIOR (*aside to* Humphrey).

Are you sure of that?

HUMPHREY (*aside*).

How he likes being prevented.

SIR JOHN BEVIL (*looking on his watch*).

No, no. You are an hour or two too early.

BEVIL JUNIOR.

You'll allow me, sir, to think it too late to visit a beautiful,

---

85. *chair*] sedan chair.

virtuous young woman in the pride and bloom of life, ready 95
to give herself to my arms; and to place her happiness or
misery for the future in being agreeable or displeasing to me
is a—call a chair.

SIR JOHN BEVIL.

No, no, no, dear Jack; this Sealand is a moody old fellow.
There's no dealing with some people but by managing with 100
indifference. We must leave to him the conduct of this day.
It is the last of his commanding his daughter.

BEVIL JUNIOR.

Sir, he can't take it ill that I am impatient to be hers.

SIR JOHN BEVIL.

Pray let me govern in this matter. You can't tell how
humorsome old fellows are. There's no offering reason to 105
some of 'em, especially when they are rich. (*Aside.*) If my
son should see him before I've brought old Sealand into better temper, the match would be impracticable.

HUMPHREY.

Pray, sir, let me beg you to let Mr. Bevil go. (*Aside to* Sir
John Bevil.) See whether he will or not. (*Then to* Bevil 110
Junior.) Pray, sir, command yourself; since you see my
master is positive, it is better you should not go.

BEVIL JUNIOR.

My father commands me as to the object of my affections,
but I hope he will not as to the warmth and height of them.

SIR JOHN BEVIL [*aside*].

So! I must even leave things as I found them. And in the 115
meantime, at least, keep old Sealand out of his sight. —Well,
son, I'll go myself and take orders in your affair. You'll be in
the way, I suppose, if I send to you. I'll leave your old friend
with you. [*Aside to* Humphrey.] Humphrey, don't let
him stir, d'ye hear? —Your servant, your servant. 120

Exit Sir John Bevil.

HUMPHREY.

I have a sad time on't, sir, between you and my master. I
see you are unwilling, and I know his violent inclinations for
the match. I must betray neither and yet deceive you both
for your common good. Heav'n grant a good end of this
matter. But there is a lady, sir, that gives your father much 125
trouble and sorrow—you'll pardon me.

BEVIL JUNIOR.

Humphrey, I know thou art a friend to both, and in that confidence, I dare tell thee—that lady—is a woman of honor and virtue. You may assure yourself I never will marry without my father's consent. But give me leave to say too, this 130 declaration does not come up to a promise that I will take whomsoever he pleases.

HUMPHREY.

Come, sir, I wholly understand you. You would engage my services to free you from this woman whom my master intends you, to make way, in time, for the woman you have 135 really a mind to.

BEVIL JUNIOR.

Honest Humphrey, you have always been an useful friend to my father and myself; I beg you continue your good offices, and don't let us come to the necessity of a dispute; for, if we should dispute, I must either part with more than life or lose 140 the best of fathers.

HUMPHREY.

My dear master, were I but worthy to know this secret that so near concerns you, my life, my all should be engaged to serve you. This, sir, I dare promise, that I am sure I will and can be secret. Your trust, at worst, but leaves you where you 145 were; and if I cannot serve you, I will at once be plain and tell you so.

BEVIL JUNIOR.

That's all I ask. Thou hast made it now my interest to trust thee. Be patient then, and hear the story of my heart.

HUMPHREY.

I am all attention, sir. 150

BEVIL JUNIOR.

You may remember, Humphrey, that in my last travels my father grew uneasy at my making so long a stay at Toulon.

HUMPHREY.

I remember it; he was apprehensive some woman had laid hold of you.

BEVIL JUNIOR.

His fears were just, for there I first saw this lady. She is of 155 English birth: her father's name was Danvers, a younger brother of an ancient family, and originally an eminent merchant of Bristol, who, upon repeated misfortunes, was reduced to go privately to the Indies. In this retreat Providence again grew favorable to his industry and, in six years' time, 160 restored him to his former fortunes. On this he sent directions over that his wife and little family should follow him to the Indies. His wife, impatient to obey such welcome orders, would not wait the leisure of a convoy, but took the first occasion of a single ship, and with her husband's sister only 165 and this daughter, then scarce seven years old, undertook the fatal voyage. For here, poor creature, she lost her liberty, and life; she and her family, with all they had, were unfortunately taken by a privateer from Toulon. Being thus made a prisoner, though as such not ill treated, yet the fright, the 170 shock, and cruel disappointment seized with such violence upon her unhealthy frame, she sickened, pined, and died at sea.

HUMPHREY.

Poor soul! Oh the helpless infant!

BEVIL JUNIOR.

Her sister yet survived and had the care of her. The captain 175 too proved to have humanity and became a father to her; for having himself married an English woman, and being childless, he brought home into Toulon this her little countrywoman, presenting her, with all her dead mother's movables of value, to his wife, to be educated as his own 180 adopted daughter.

HUMPHREY.

Fortune here seemed, again, to smile on her.

BEVIL JUNIOR.

Only to make her frowns more terrible. For, in his height of fortune, this captain too, her benefactor, unfortunately was killed at sea, and dying intestate, his estate fell wholly to an 185 advocate, his brother, who coming soon to take possession, there found among his other riches this blooming virgin, at his mercy.

HUMPHREY.

He durst not, sure, abuse his power!

183. his] *O1–2, D1*; this *O3*.

BEVIL JUNIOR.

No wonder if his pampered blood was fired at the sight of her—in short, he loved. But when all arts and gentle means had failed to move, he offered too his menaces in vain, denouncing vengeance on her cruelty, demanding her to account for all her maintenance from her childhood, seized on her little fortune as his own inheritance, and was dragging her by violence to prison when Providence at the instant interposed and sent me, by miracle, to relieve her. 190 195

HUMPHREY.

'Twas Providence indeed, But pray, sir, after all this trouble, how came this lady at last to England?

BEVIL JUNIOR.

The disappointed advocate, finding she had so unexpected a support, on cooler thoughts descended to a composition, which I, without her knowledge, secretly discharged. 200

HUMPHREY.

That generous concealment made the obligation double.

BEVIL JUNIOR.

Having thus obtained her liberty, I prevailed, not without some difficulty, to see her safe to England; where no sooner arrived, but my father, jealous of my being imprudently engaged, immediately proposed this other fatal match that hangs upon my quiet. 205

HUMPHREY.

I find, sir, you are irrecoverably fixed upon this lady.

BEVIL JUNIOR.

As my vital life dwells in my heart. And yet you see what I do to please my father: walk in this pageantry of dress, this splendid covering of sorrow. But, Humphrey, you have your lesson. 210

HUMPHREY.

Now, sir, I have but one material question—

BEVIL JUNIOR.

Ask it freely. 215

HUMPHREY.

Is it, then, your own passion for this secret lady or hers for

---

201. *descended to a composition*] agreed to a smaller amount of money to satisfy his alleged claim on Indiana.

you that gives you this aversion to the match your father has proposed you?

BEVIL JUNIOR.

I shall appear, Humphrey, more romantic in my answer than in all the rest of my story. For though I dote on her to death and have no little reason to believe she has the same thoughts for me, yet in all my acquaintance and utmost privacies with her, I never once directly told her that I loved. 220

HUMPHREY.

How was it possible to avoid it?

BEVIL JUNIOR.

My tender obligations to my father have laid so inviolable a restraint upon my conduct that, till I have his consent to speak, I am determined on that subject to be dumb forever. 225

HUMPHREY.

Well, sir, to your praise be it spoken, you are certainly the most unfashionable lover in Great Britain.

Enter Tom.

TOM.

Sir, Mr. Myrtle's at the next door, and if you are at leisure, will be glad to wait on you. 230

BEVIL JUNIOR.

Whenever he pleases—hold, Tom! Did you receive no answer to my letter?

TOM.

Sir, I was desired to call again; for I was told her mother would not let her be out of her sight; but about an hour hence, Mrs. Phillis said, I should certainly have one. 235

BEVIL JUNIOR.

Very well. [*Exit* Tom.]

HUMPHREY.

Sir, I will take another opportunity. In the meantime, I only think it proper to tell you that from a secret I know, you may appear to your father as forward as you please to marry Lucinda, without the least hazard of its coming to a conclusion—sir, your most obedient servant. 240

236. Phillis] *Lettice O1–3, D1. Steele obviously intended* Phillis *as the context demands.* Lettice *is the name of a serving-girl in* The Lying Lover.

BEVIL JUNIOR.

Honest Humphrey, continue but my friend in this exigence, and you shall always find me yours. *Exit* Humphrey.
I long to hear how my letter has succeeded with Lucinda. 245
But I think it cannot fail; for, at worst, were it possible she could take it ill, her resentment of my indifference may as probably occasion a delay as her taking it right. Poor Myrtle, what terrors must he be in all this while? Since he knows she is offered to me and refused to him, there is no conversing or 250
taking any measures with him for his own service. But I ought to bear with my friend and use him as one in adversity:

All his disquiets by my own I prove,
The greatest grief's perplexity in love. *Exit.* 255

251. But] *O2–3, D1*; But But *O1.* 255. *Exit*] *Exeunt O1–3, D1.*

ACT II

[II.i] *Scene continues. Enter* Bevil Junior *and* Tom.

TOM.
Sir, Mr. Myrtle.

BEVIL JUNIOR.
Very well, do you step again and wait for an answer to my letter. [*Exit* Tom.]

Enter Myrtle.

Well, Charles, why so much care in thy countenance? Is there anything in this world deserves it? You, who used to be 5
so gay, so open, so vacant!

MYRTLE.
I think we have of late changed complexions. You, who used to be much the graver man, are now all air in your behavior. But the cause of my concern may, for aught I know, be the same object that gives you all this satisfaction. In a word, I 10
am told that you are this very day—and your dress confirms me in it—to be married to Lucinda.

BEVIL JUNIOR.
You are not misinformed. Nay, put not on the terrors of a rival till you hear me out. I shall disoblige the best of fathers if I don't seem ready to marry Lucinda. And you know I 15
have ever told you, you might make use of my secret resolution never to marry her, for your own service, as you please. But I am now driven to the extremity of immediately refusing or complying unless you help me to escape the match.

MYRTLE.
Escape? Sir, neither her merit or her fortune are below your 20
acceptance. Escaping, do you call it!

BEVIL JUNIOR.
Dear sir, do you wish I should desire the match?

MYRTLE.
No—but such is my humorous and sickly state of mind, since it has been able to relish nothing but Lucinda, that though

---

6. *open*] unreserved.
6. *vacant*] at leisure.

I must owe my happiness to your aversion to this marriage, 25
I can't bear to hear her spoken of with levity or unconcern.

BEVIL JUNIOR.
Pardon me, sir; I shall transgress that way no more. She has understanding, beauty, shape, complexion, wit—

MYRTLE.
Nay, dear Bevil, don't speak of her as if you loved her, neither. 30

BEVIL JUNIOR.
Why then, to give you ease at once, though I allow Lucinda to have good sense, wit, beauty, and virtue, I know another in whom these qualities appear to me more amiable than in her.

MYRTLE.
There you spoke like a reasonable and good-natured friend. 35
When you acknowledge her merit and own your prepossession for another at once, you gratify my fondness and cure my jealousy.

BEVIL JUNIOR.
But all this while you take no notice, you have no apprehension of another man that has twice the fortune of either of us. 40

MYRTLE.
Cimberton! Hang him, a formal, philosophical, pedantic coxcomb! For the sot, with all these crude notions of diverse things, under the direction of great vanity and very little judgment, shows his strongest bias is avarice, which is so predominant in him that he will examine the limbs of his 45
mistress with the caution of a jockey and pays no more compliment to her personal charms than if she were a mere breeding animal.

BEVIL JUNIOR.
Are you sure that is not affected? I have known some women sooner set on fire by that sort of negligence than by— 50

MYRTLE.
No, no; hang him, the rogue has no art; it is pure simple insolence and stupidity.

BEVIL JUNIOR.
Yet, with all this, I don't take him for a fool.

53. a] *O1–3*; *om. D1.*

MYRTLE.

I own the man is not a natural; he has a very quick sense, though very slow understanding. He says indeed many things that want only the circumstances of time and place to be very just and agreeable. 55

BEVIL JUNIOR.

Well, you may be sure of me if you can disappoint him; but my intelligence says the mother has actually sent for the conveyancer to draw articles for his marriage with Lucinda, though those for mine with her are, by her father's order, ready for signing; but it seems she has not thought fit to consult either him or his daughter in the matter. 60

MYRTLE.

Pshaw! A poor troublesome woman. Neither Lucinda nor her father will ever be brought to comply with it. Besides, I am sure Cimberton can make no settlement upon her without the concurrence of his great uncle Sir Geoffry in the West. 65

BEVIL JUNIOR.

Well sir, and I can tell you, that's the very point that is now laid before her counsel, to know whether a firm settlement can be made without this uncle's actual joining in it. Now pray consider, sir, when my affair with Lucinda comes, as it soon must, to an open rupture, how are you sure that Cimberton's fortune may not then tempt her father too to hear his proposals? 70

MYRTLE.

There you are right indeed, that must be provided against. Do you know who are her counsel? 75

BEVIL JUNIOR.

Yes, for your service I have found out that too; they are Serjeant Bramble and old Target. By the way, they are neither of 'em known in the family; now I was thinking why you might not put a couple of false counsel upon her to delay and confound matters a little. Besides, it may probably let you into the bottom of her whole design against you. 80

---

54. *natural*] half-wit.

60. *conveyancer*] a lawyer who prepares documents for the conveyance of property.

78. *Serjeant*] a title denoting membership in a superior order of barristers.

MYRTLE.

As how, pray?

BEVIL JUNIOR.

Why, can't you slip on a black wig and a gown and be old Bramble yourself? 85

MYRTLE.

Ha! I don't dislike it—but what shall I do for a brother in the case?

BEVIL JUNIOR.

What think you of my fellow, Tom? The rogue's intelligent and is a good mimic; all his part will be but to stutter heartily, for that's old Target's case. Nay, it would be an immoral 90 thing to mock him, were it not that his impertinence is the occasion of its breaking out to that degree. The conduct of the scene will chiefly lie upon you.

MYRTLE.

I like it of all things. If you'll send Tom to my chambers, I will give him full instructions. This will certainly give me 95 occasion to raise difficulties, to puzzle or confound her project for a while at least.

BEVIL JUNIOR.

I'll warrant you success. So far we are right then. And now, Charles, your apprehension of my marrying her is all you have to get over. 100

MYRTLE.

Dear Bevil! Though I know you are my friend, yet when I abstract myself from my own interest in the thing, I know no objection she can make to you or you to her, and therefore hope—

BEVIL JUNIOR.

Dear Myrtle, I am as much obliged to you for the cause of 105 your suspicion as I am offended at the effect. But be assured, I am taking measures for your certain security and that all things with regard to me will end in your entire satisfaction.

MYRTLE (*going*).

Well, I'll promise you to be as easy and as confident as I can, though I cannot but remember that I have more than life at 110 stake on your fidelity.

---

96. *puzzle*] complicate, entangle.

BEVIL JUNIOR.

Then depend upon it, you have no chance against you.

MYRTLE.

Nay, no ceremony, you know I must be going. *Exit* Myrtle.

BEVIL JUNIOR.

Well! This is another instance of the perplexities which arise too in faithful friendship. We must often, in this life, go 115 on in our good offices even under the displeasure of those to whom we do them, in compassion to their weaknesses and mistakes. But all this while poor Indiana is tortured with the doubt of me! She has no support or comfort but in my fidelity, yet sees me daily pressed to marriage with another! How 120 painful, in such a crisis, must be every hour she thinks on me! I'll let her see, at least, my conduct to her is not changed. I'll take this opportunity to visit her; for though the religious vow I have made to my father restrains me from ever marrying without his approbation, yet that confines me not 125 from seeing a virtuous woman that is the pure delight of my eyes and the guiltless joy of my heart. But the best condition of human life is but a gentler misery.

To hope for perfect happiness is vain,
And Love has ever its allays of pain. *Exit.* 130

[II.ii] *Enter* Isabella *and* Indiana *in her own lodgings.*

ISABELLA.

Yes, I say 'tis artifice, dear child; I say to thee again and again, 'tis all skill and management.

INDIANA.

Will you persuade me there can be an ill design in supporting me in the condition of a woman of quality? Attended, dressed, and lodged like one; in my appearance abroad and 5 my furniture at home, every way in the most sumptuous manner, and he that does it has an artifice, a design in it?

ISABELLA.

Yes, yes.

INDIANA.

And all this without so much as explaining to me that all about me comes from him? 10

130. *allays*] alloys.

ISABELLA.

Ay, ay, the more for that—that keeps the title to all you have the more in him.

INDIANA.

The more in him! He scorns the thought—

ISABELLA.

Then he—he—he—

INDIANA.

Well, be not so eager. If he is an ill man, let us look into his stratagems. Here is another of them. (*Showing a letter.*) Here's two hundred and fifty pound in bank notes with these words, "To pay for the set of dressing-plate, which will be brought home tomorrow." Why, dear aunt, now here's another piece of skill for you which I own I cannot comprehend; and it is with a bleeding heart I hear you say anything to the disadvantage of Mr. Bevil. When he is present, I look upon him as one to whom I owe my life and the support of it, then again, as the man who loves me with sincerity and honor. When his eyes are cast another way and I dare survey him, my heart is painfully divided between shame and love. Oh, could I tell you— 15 20 25

ISABELLA.

Ah, you need not. I imagine all this for you.

INDIANA.

This is my state of mind in his presence; and when he is absent, you are ever dinning my ears with notions of the arts of men; that his hidden bounty, his respectful conduct, his careful provision for me after his preserving me from utmost misery are certain signs he means nothing but to make I know not what of me. 30

ISABELLA.

Oh! You have a sweet opinion of him, truly. 35

INDIANA.

I have, when I am with him, ten thousand things besides my sex's natural decency and shame to suppress my heart that yearns to thank, to praise, to say it loves him. I say, thus it is with me while I see him; and in his absence I am entertained with nothing but your endeavors to tear this amiable 40

18. *dressing-plate*] silver toilet service.

image from my heart and, in its stead, to place a base dissembler, an artful invader of my happiness, my innocence, my honor.

ISABELLA.

Ah, poor soul! Has not his plot taken? Don't you die for him? Has not the way he has taken been the most proper with you? 45 Oh ho! He has sense and has judged the thing right.

INDIANA.

Go on then, since nothing can answer you; say what you will of him. Heigh ho!

ISABELLA.

Heigh ho, indeed. It is better to say so as you are now than as many others are. There are, among the destroyers of 50 women, the gentle, the generous, the mild, the affable, the humble, who all, soon after their success in their designs, turn to the contrary of those characters. I will own to you Mr. Bevil carries his hypocrisy the best of any man living, but still he is a man and therefore a hypocrite. They have 55 usurped an exemption from shame for any baseness, any cruelty towards us. They embrace without love; they make vows without conscience of obligation; they are partners, nay, seducers to the crime wherein they pretend to be less guilty. 60

INDIANA (*aside*).

That's truly observed. —But what's all this to Bevil?

ISABELLA.

This it is to Bevil and all mankind. Trust not those who will think the worse of you for your confidence in them. Serpents who lie in wait for doves! Won't you be on your guard against those who would betray you? Won't you doubt those who 65 would contemn you for believing 'em? Take it from me, fair and natural dealing is to invite injuries; 'tis bleating to escape wolves who would devour you. Such is the world— (*aside*) and such, since the behavior of one man to myself, have I believed all the rest of the sex. 70

INDIANA.

I will not doubt the truth of Bevil, I will not doubt it. He has

46. ho] *O1–3*; oh *D1.*

46. thing right] *O1–2*, *D1*; right thing *O3.*

not spoken it by an organ that is given to lying: his eyes are all that have ever told me that he was mine. I know his virtue, I know his filial piety, and ought to trust his management with a father to whom he has uncommon obligations. What 75 have I to be concerned for? My lesson is very short. If he takes me forever, my purpose of life is only to please him. If he leaves me, which Heaven avert, I know he'll do it nobly, and I shall have nothing to do but to learn to die after worse than death has happened to me. 80

ISABELLA.

Ay do, persist in your credulity! Flatter yourself that a man of his figure and fortune will make himself the jest of the town and marry a handsome beggar for love.

INDIANA.

The town! I must tell you, madam, the fools that laugh at Mr. Bevil will but make themselves more ridiculous. His 85 actions are the result of thinking, and he has sense enough to make even virtue fashionable.

ISABELLA.

O' my conscience he has turned her head. —Come, come; if he were the honest fool you take him for, why has he kept you here these three weeks without sending you to Bristol in 90 search of your father, your family, and your relations?

INDIANA.

I am convinced he still designs it and that nothing keeps him here but the necessity of not coming to a breach with his father in regard to the match he has proposed him. Beside, has he not writ to Bristol? And has not he advice that my 95 father has not been heard of there almost these twenty years?

ISABELLA.

All sham, mere evasion; he is afraid if he should carry you thither, your honest relations may take you out of his hands and so blow up all his wicked hopes at once.

INDIANA.

Wicked hopes! Did I ever give him any such? 100

ISABELLA.

Has he ever given you any honest ones? Can you say, in your conscience, he has ever once offered to marry you?

---

82. *the town*] i.e., fashionable London.

INDIANA.

No! But by his behavior I am convinced he will offer it the moment 'tis in his power or consistent with his honor to make such a promise good to me. 105

ISABELLA.

His honor!

INDIANA.

I will rely upon it; therefore desire you will not make my life uneasy by these ungrateful jealousies of one to whom I am and wish to be obliged. For from his integrity alone I have resolved to hope for happiness. 110

ISABELLA.

Nay, I have done my duty; if you won't see, at your peril be it—

INDIANA.

Let it be. This is his hour of visiting me.

ISABELLA.

Oh, to be sure, keep up your form; don't see him in a bed-chamber. (*Apart.*) This is pure prudence when she is 115 liable, wherever he meets her, to be conveyed where'er he pleases.

INDIANA.

All the rest of my life is but waiting till he comes. I live only when I'm with him. *Exit.*

ISABELLA.

Well, go thy ways, thou willful innocent! I once had almost 120 as much love for a man who poorly left me to marry an estate. And I am now, against my will, what they call an old maid. But I will not let the peevishness of that condition grow upon me, only keep up the suspicion of it, to prevent this creature's being any other than a virgin except upon 125 proper terms. *Exit.*

Re-enter Indiana, *speaking to a Servant.*

INDIANA.

Desire Mr. Bevil to walk in. [*Exit Servant.*]
Design! Impossible! A base, designing mind could never think of what he hourly puts in practice. And yet, since the

---

121. *poorly*] basely.

late rumor of his marriage, he seems more reserved than 130
formerly. He sends in, too, before he sees me, to know if I
am at leisure. Such new respect may cover coldness in the
heart. It certainly makes me thoughtful. I'll know the worst
at once; I'll lay such fair occasions in his way that it shall be
impossible to avoid an explanation. For these doubts are in- 135
supportable! But see, he comes, and clears them all.

Enter Bevil Junior.

BEVIL JUNIOR.
Madam, your most obedient—I am afraid I broke in upon
your rest last night. 'Twas very late before we parted, but
'twas your own fault: I never saw you in such agreeable
humor. 140

INDIANA.
I am extremely glad we were both pleased, for I thought I
never saw you better company.

BEVIL JUNIOR.
Me, madam! You rally. I said very little.

INDIANA.
But I am afraid you heard me say a great deal; and when
a woman is in the talking vein, the most agreeable thing a 145
man can do, you know, is to have patience to hear her.

BEVIL JUNIOR.
Then it's pity, madam, you should ever be silent, that we
might be always agreeable to one another.

INDIANA.
If I had your talent or power to make my actions speak for
me, I might indeed be silent and yet pretend to something 150
more than the agreeable.

BEVIL JUNIOR.
If I might be vain of anything in my power, madam, 'tis
that my understanding from all your sex has marked you out
as the most deserving object of my esteem.

INDIANA.
Should I think I deserve this, 'twere enough to make my 155
vanity forfeit the very esteem you offer me.

BEVIL JUNIOR.
How so, madam?

INDIANA.

Because esteem is the result of reason, and to deserve it from good sense, the height of human glory. Nay, I had rather a man of honor should pay me that than all the homage of a sincere and humble love. 160

BEVIL JUNIOR.

You certainly distinguish right, madam; love often kindles from external merit only—

INDIANA.

But esteem arises from a higher source, the merit of the soul—

BEVIL JUNIOR.

True. And great souls only can deserve it. 165

Bowing respectfully

INDIANA.

Now I think they are greater still that can so charitably part with it.

BEVIL JUNIOR.

Now, madam, you make me vain since the utmost pride and pleasure of my life is that I esteem you—as I ought.

INDIANA (*aside*).

As he ought! Still more perplexing! He neither saves nor kills my hope. 170

BEVIL JUNIOR.

But madam, we grow grave methinks. Let's find some other subject. Pray, how did you like the opera last night?

INDIANA.

First give me leave to thank you for my tickets.

BEVIL JUNIOR.

Oh, your servant, madam. But pray tell me, you now who are never partial to the fashion I fancy must be the properest judge of a mighty dispute among the ladies, that is, whether *Crispo* or *Griselda* is the more agreeable entertainment. 175

INDIANA.

With submission now, I cannot be a proper judge of this question. 180

---

178. *Crispo or Griselda*] two popular operas by Giovanni Battista Bononcini with libretto by Paolo Antonio Rolli performed at the King's Theatre in 1722. *Crispus* ran for eighteen nights, *Griselda* for sixteen nights before *The Conscious Lovers* opened in November.

BEVIL JUNIOR.

How so, madam?

INDIANA.

Because I find I have a partiality for one of them.

BEVIL JUNIOR.

Pray, which is that?

INDIANA.

I do not know—there's something in that rural cottage of Griselda, her forlorn condition, her poverty, her solitude, her resignation, her innocent slumbers, and that lulling "*Dolce Sogno*" that's sung over her; it had an effect upon me that—in short, I never was so well deceived at any of them. 185

BEVIL JUNIOR.

Oh! Now then, I can account for the dispute: *Griselda*, it seems, is the distress of an injured innocent woman; *Crispo*, that only of a man in the same condition. Therefore the men are mostly concerned for Crispo, and, by a natural indulgence, both sexes for Griselda. 190

INDIANA.

So that judgment, you think, ought to be for one though fancy and complaisance have got ground for the other. Well, I believe you will never give me leave to dispute with you on any subject, for I own *Crispo* has its charms for me too, though in the main, all the pleasure the best opera gives us is but mere sensation. Methinks it's pity the mind can't have a little more share in the entertainment. The music's certainly fine, but in my thoughts there's none of your composers come up to old Shakespeare and Otway. 195 200

BEVIL JUNIOR.

How, madam! Why if a woman of your sense were to say this in the drawing room— 205

Enter a Servant.

SERVANT.

Sir, here's Signor Carbonelli says he waits your commands in the next room.

---

188. "*Dolce Sogno*"] "Sweet Dream." Persecuted by evil-wishers, Griselda, a shepherdess who has married the king of Sicily, hides in a rural cottage where her husband finds her sleeping and sings this song.

BEVIL JUNIOR.

A propos! You were saying yesterday, madam, you had a mind to hear him. Will you give him leave to entertain you now? 210

INDIANA.

By all means. Desire the gentleman to walk in.

Exit Servant.

BEVIL JUNIOR.

I fancy you will find something in this hand that is uncommon.

INDIANA.

You are always finding ways, Mr. Bevil, to make life seem less tedious to me. 215

Enter Music Master.

When the gentleman pleases.

After a sonata is played, Bevil Junior *waits on the Master to the door, etc.*

BEVIL JUNIOR.

You smile, madam, to see me so complaisant to one whom I pay for his visit. Now I own I think it is not enough barely to pay those whose talents are superior to our own—I mean such talents as would become our condition if we had them. 220 Methinks we ought to do something more than barely gratify them for what they do at our command only because their fortune is below us.

INDIANA.

You say I smile. I assure you it was a smile of approbation, for indeed I cannot but think it the distinguishing part of a 225 gentleman to make his superiority of fortune as easy to his inferiors as he can. (*Aside.*) Now once more to try him. —I was saying just now I believed you would never let me dispute with you, and I dare say it will always be so. However I must have your opinion upon a subject which created 230 a debate between my aunt and me just before you came hither. She would needs have it that no man ever does any extraordinary kindness or service for a woman but for his own sake.

221–222. *gratify*] pay.

BEVIL JUNIOR.

Well, madam! Indeed I can't but be of her mind. 235

INDIANA.

What, though he should maintain and support her without demanding anything of her on her part?

BEVIL JUNIOR.

Why, madam, is making an expense in the service of a valuable woman—for such I must suppose her—though she should never do him any favor, nay, though she should 240 never know who did her such service, such a mighty heroic business?

INDIANA.

Certainly! I should think he must be a man of an uncommon mold.

BEVIL JUNIOR.

Dear madam, why so? 'Tis but, at best, a better taste in ex- 245 pense. To bestow upon one whom he may think one of the ornaments of the whole creation, to be conscious that from his superfluity an innocent, a virtuous spirit is supported above the temptations and sorrows of life! That he sees satisfaction, health, and gladness in her countenance while he 250 enjoys the happiness of seeing her—as that I will suppose too, or he must be too abstracted, too insensible. I say, if he is allowed to delight in that prospect, alas, what mighty matter is there in all this?

INDIANA.

No mighty matter in so disinterested a friendship! 255

BEVIL JUNIOR.

Disinterested! I can't think him so. Your hero, madam, is no more than what every gentleman ought to be, and I believe very many are. He is only one who takes more delight in reflections than in sensations. He is more pleased with thinking than eating. That's the utmost you can say of him. 260 Why, madam, a greater expense than all this men lay out upon an unnecessary stable of horses.

INDIANA.

Can you be sincere in what you say?

BEVIL JUNIOR.

You may depend upon it, if you know any such man, he does not love dogs inordinately. 265

INDIANA.

No, that he does not.

BEVIL JUNIOR.

Nor cards, nor dice.

INDIANA.

No.

BEVIL JUNIOR.

Nor bottle companions.

INDIANA.

No. 270

BEVIL JUNIOR.

Nor loose women.

INDIANA.

No, I'm sure he does not.

BEVIL JUNIOR.

Take my word then, if your admired hero is not liable to any of these kinds of demands, there's no such pre-eminence in this as you imagine. Nay, this way of expense you speak of is 275 what exalts and raises him that has a taste for it. And at the same time his delight is incapable of satiety, disgust, or penitence.

INDIANA.

But still I insist his having no private interest in the action makes it prodigious, almost incredible. 280

BEVIL JUNIOR.

Dear madam, I never knew you more mistaken. Why, who can be more an usurer than he who lays out his money in such valuable purchases? If pleasure be worth purchasing, how great a pleasure is it to him who has a true taste of life to ease an aching heart, to see the human countenance lighted 285 up into smiles of joy on the receipt of a bit of ore which is superfluous and otherwise useless in a man's own pocket? What could a man do better with his cash? This is the effect of an humane disposition where there is only a general tie of nature and common necessity. What then must it be when 290 we serve an object of merit, of admiration!

274. these] *O1, D1*; those *O2–3*. 285. human] *O2–3*; humane *O1, D1*.

289. *humane*] courteous, friendly.

INDIANA.

Well, the more you argue against it, the more I shall admire the generosity.

BEVIL JUNIOR.

Nay, nay. Then, madam, 'tis time to fly, after a declaration that my opinion strengthens my adversary's argument. I 295 had best hasten to my appointment with Mr. Myrtle and begone while we are friends and—before things are brought to an extremity— *Exit carelessly.*

Enter Isabella.

ISABELLA.

Well, madam, what think you of him now, pray?

INDIANA.

I protest I begin to fear he is wholly disinterested in what he 300 does for me. On my heart, he has no other view but the mere pleasure of doing it and has neither good or bad designs upon me.

ISABELLA.

Ah, dear niece! Don't be in fear of both! I'll warrant you, you will know time enough that he is not indifferent. 305

INDIANA.

You please me when you tell me so. For if he has any wishes towards me, I know he will not pursue them but with honor.

ISABELLA.

I wish I were as confident of one as t'other. I saw the respectful downcast of his eye when you catcht him gazing at you during the music. He, I warrant, was surprised, as if he 310 had been taken stealing your watch. Oh, the undissembled guilty look!

INDIANA.

But did you observe any such thing, really? I thought he looked most charmingly graceful! How engaging is modesty in a man when one knows there is a great mind within. So 315 tender a confusion! And yet, in other respects, so much himself, so collected, so dauntless, so determined!

ISABELLA.

Ah, niece! There is a sort of bashfulness which is the best engine to carry on a shameless purpose. Some men's modesty serves their wickedness, as hypocrisy gains the respect due 320 to piety. But I will own to you, there is one hopeful symptom, if there could be such a thing as a disinterested lover. But it's all a perplexity, till—till—till—

INDIANA.

Till what?

ISABELLA.

Till I know whether Mr. Myrtle and Mr. Bevil are really friends or foes. And that I will be convinced of before I sleep, for you shall not be deceived. 325

INDIANA.

I'm sure I never shall if your fears can guard me. In the meantime, I'll wrap myself up in the integrity of my own heart, nor dare to doubt of his. 330

As conscious honor all his actions steers:
So conscious innocence dispels my fears. *Exeunt.*

ACT III

Scene, Sealand's house. Enter Tom *meeting* Phillis.

TOM.

Well, Phillis! What, with a face as if you had never seen me before? (*Aside.*) What a work have I to do now! She has seen some new visitant at their house whose airs she has catched and is resolved to practice them upon me. Numberless are the changes she'll dance through before she'll answer this plain question, *videlicit*, have you delivered my master's letter to your lady? Nay, I know her too well to ask an account of it in an ordinary way; I'll be in my airs as well as she. —Well, madam, as unhappy as you are at present pleased to make me, I would not, in the general, be any other than what I am. I would not be a bit wiser, a bit richer, a bit taller, a bit shorter than I am at this instant. 5 10

Looking steadfastly at her

PHILLIS.

Did ever anybody doubt, Master Thomas, but that you were extremely satisfied with your sweet self?

TOM.

I am indeed. The thing I have least reason to be satisfied with is my fortune, and I am glad of my poverty. Perhaps if I were rich, I should overlook the finest woman in the world that wants nothing but riches to be thought so. 15

PHILLIS (*aside*).

How prettily was that said! But I'll have a great deal more before I'll say one word. 20

TOM.

I should, perhaps, have been stupidly above her, had I not been her equal; and by not being her equal, never had opportunity of being her slave. I am my master's servant for hire; I am my mistress's from choice, would she but approve my passion. 25

PHILLIS.

I think it's the first time I ever heard you speak of it with any sense of the anguish, if you really do suffer any.

TOM.

Ah, Phillis, can you doubt, after what you have seen?

PHILLIS.

I know not what I have seen, nor what I have heard. But since I'm at leisure, you may tell me when you fell in love with me, how you fell in love with me, and what you have suffered or are ready to suffer for me. 30

TOM (*aside*).

Oh, the unmerciful jade! When I'm in haste about my master's letter! But I must go through it. —Ah! Too well I remember when and how and on what occasion I was first surprised. It was on the first of April, one thousand seven hundred and fifteen, I came into Mr. Sealand's service. I was then a hobbledehoy, and you a pretty little tight girl, a favorite handmaid of the housekeeper. At that time, we neither of us knew what was in us. I remember I was ordered to get out of the window, one pair of stairs, to rub the sashes clean. The person employed on the innerside was your charming self, whom I had never seen before. 35 40

PHILLIS.

I think I remember the silly accident. What made ye, you oaf, ready to fall down into the street? 45

TOM.

You know not, I warrant you. You could not guess what surprised me. You took no delight when you immediately grew wanton in your conquest and put your lips close and breathed upon the glass, and when my lips approached, a dirty cloth you rubbed against my face and hid your beauteous form; when I again drew near, you spit and rubbed and smiled at my undoing. 50

PHILLIS.

What silly thoughts you men have!

TOM.

We were Pyramus and Thisbe. But ten times harder was my fate. Pyramus could peep only through a wall; I saw her, saw my Thisbe in all her beauty but as much kept from her 55

---

38. *tight*] lively.
41. *one . . . stairs*] on the second floor.
47–52. *You . . . undoing*] See the *Guardian*, No. 87, for Steele's first description of this incident.

as if a hundred walls between, for there was more, there was her will against me. Would she but yet relent! Oh, Phillis! Phillis! Shorten my torment and declare you pity me.

PHILLIS.

I believe it's very sufferable; the pain is not so exquisite but that you may bear it a little longer. 60

TOM.

Oh, my charming Phillis, if all depended on my fair one's will, I could with glory suffer. But, dearest creature, consider our miserable state.

PHILLIS.

How! Miserable! 65

TOM.

We are miserable to be in love and under the command of others than those we love—with that generous passion in the heart, to be sent to and fro on errands, called, checked and rated for the meanest trifles. Oh, Phillis! You don't know how many china cups and glasses my passion for you has made me break. You have broke my fortune as well as my heart. 70

PHILLIS.

Well, Mr. Thomas, I cannot but own to you that I believe your master writes and you speak the best of any men in the world. Never was woman so well pleased with a letter as my young lady was with his, and this is an answer to it. 75

Gives him a letter.

TOM.

This was well done, my dearest. Consider, we must strike out some pretty livelihood for ourselves by closing their affairs. It will be nothing for them to give us a little being of our own, some small tenement out of their large possessions. Whatever they give us, 'twill be more than what they keep for themselves: one acre, with Phillis, would be worth a whole county without her. 80

PHILLIS.

O, could I but believe you!

68–69. *checked and rated*] reprimanded.
79. *being*] livelihood.
80. *tenement*] property.

TOM.

If not the utterance, believe the touch of my lips. 85

Kisses her.

PHILLIS.

There's no contradicting you. How closely you argue, Tom!

TOM.

And will closer, in due time. But I must hasten with this letter, to hasten toward the possession of you. Then, Phillis, consider how I must be revenged, look to it, of all your skittishness, shy looks, and at best but coy compliances. 90

PHILLIS.

Oh, Tom, you grow wanton and sensual, as my lady calls it; I must not endure it. Oh! Foh! You are a man, an odious filthy male creature. You should behave, if you had a right sense or were a man of sense like Mr. Cimberton, with distance and indifference, or, let me see, some other becoming 95 hard word, with seeming in-in-inadvertency, and not rush on one as if you were seizing a prey. But hush—the ladies are coming. Good Tom, don't kiss me above once and be gone. Lard, we have been fooling and toying and not considered the main business of our masters and mistresses. 100

TOM.

Why, their business is to be fooling and toying as soon as the parchments are ready.

PHILLIS.

Well remembered—parchments. My lady, to my knowledge, is preparing writings between her coxcomb cousin Cimberton and my mistress though my master has an eye to the 105 parchments already prepared between your master Mr. Bevil and my mistress; and I believe my mistress herself has signed and sealed, in her heart, to Mr. Myrtle—did I not bid you kiss me but once and be gone? But I know you won't be satisfied. 110

TOM.

No, you smooth creature, how should I! *Kissing her hand.*

98. Good] *O2–3, D1*; God *O1.*

---

86. *closely*] pithily; here there is a pun on Tom's physical proximity.

90. *coy*] modest.

102. *parchments*] marriage contracts.

PHILLIS.

Well, since you are so humble, or so cool, as to ravish my hand only, I'll take my leave of you like a great lady, and you a man of quality. *They salute formally.*

TOM.

Pox of all this state. *Offers to kiss her more closely.* 115

PHILLIS.

No, prithee, Tom, mind your business. We must follow that interest which will take, but endeavor at that which will be most for us and we like most. Oh, here's my young mistress! (Tom *taps her neck behind and kisses his fingers.*) Go, ye liquorish fool. *Exit* Tom. 120

Enter Lucinda.

LUCINDA.

Who was that you was hurrying away?

PHILLIS.

One that I had no mind to part with.

LUCINDA.

Why did you turn him away then?

PHILLIS.

For your ladyship's service, to carry your ladyship's letter to his master. I could hardly get the rogue away. 125

LUCINDA.

Why, has he so little love for his master?

PHILLIS.

No, but he has so much love for his mistress.

LUCINDA.

But I thought I heard him kiss you. Why do you suffer that?

PHILLIS.

Why, madam, we vulgar take it to be a sign of love. We servants, we poor people that have nothing but our persons to 130 bestow or treat for are forced to deal and bargain by way of sample. And therefore, as we have no parchments or wax necessary in our agreements, we squeeze with our hands and seal with our lips to ratify vows and promises.

126. has he] *O1–2, D1*; he has *O3.*

---

114. S.D. *salute*] kiss.
117. *take*] succeed. 120. *liquorish*] lustful.

LUCINDA.

But can't you trust one another without such earnest down? 135

PHILLIS.

We don't think it safe, any more than you gentry, to come together without deeds executed.

LUCINDA.

Thou art a pert, merry hussy.

PHILLIS.

I wish, madam, your lover and you were as happy as Tom and your servant are. 140

LUCINDA.

You grow impertinent.

PHILLIS.

I have done, madam, and I won't ask you what you intend to do with Mr. Myrtle, what your father will do with Mr. Bevil, nor what you all, especially my lady, mean by admitting Mr. Cimberton as particularly here as if he were married to you already. Nay, you are married actually as far as people of quality are. 145

LUCINDA.

How's that?

PHILLIS.

You have different beds in the same house.

LUCINDA.

Pshaw! I have a very great value for Mr. Bevil but have absolutely put an end to his pretensions in the letter I gave you for him. But my father, in his heart, still has a mind to him, were it not for this woman they talk of. And I am apt to imagine he is married to her, or never designs to marry at all. 150 155

PHILLIS.

Then Mr. Myrtle—

LUCINDA.

He had my parents' leave to apply to me, and by that has won me and my affections; who is to have this body of mine without 'em, it seems, is nothing to me. My mother says it's indecent for me to let my thoughts stray about the person of my husband. Nay, she says a maid rigidly virtuous, though 160

159. it's] *O1–3*; 'tis *D1*.

she may have been where her lover was a thousand times, should not have made observations enough to know him from another man when she sees him in a third place.

PHILLIS.

That is more than the severity of a nun, for not to see when one may is hardly possible; not to see when one can't is very easy. At this rate, madam, there are a great many whom you have not seen who— 165

LUCINDA.

Mamma says the first time you see your husband should be at that instant he is made so, when your father with the help of the minister gives you to him; then you are to see him, then you are to observe and take notice of him, because then you are to obey him. 170

PHILLIS.

But does not my lady remember you are to love as well as obey? 175

LUCINDA.

To love is a passion, 'tis a desire, and we must have no desires. Oh, I cannot endure the reflection! With what insensibility on my part, with what more than patience have I been exposed and offered to some awkward booby or other in every county of Great Britain! 180

PHILLIS.

Indeed, madam, I wonder I never heard you speak of it before with this indignation.

LUCINDA.

Every corner of the land has presented me with a wealthy coxcomb. As fast as one treaty has gone off, another has come on, till my name and person have been the tittle-tattle of the whole town. What is this world come to? No shame left! To be bartered for like the beasts of the fields, and that in such an instance as coming together to an entire familiarity and union of soul and body. Oh! And this without being so much as well-wishers to each other but for increase of fortune. 185 190

PHILLIS.

But, madam, all these vexations will end very soon in one for all. Mr. Cimberton is your mother's kinsman and three hundred years an older gentleman than any lover you ever had, for which reason, with that of his prodigious large estate, she is resolved on him and has sent to consult the lawyers accordingly. Nay, has, whether you know it or no, been in treaty with Sir Geoffry, who, to join in the settlement, has accepted of a sum to do it and is every moment expected in town for that purpose. 195 200

LUCINDA.
How do you get all this intelligence?

PHILLIS.
By an art I have, I thank my stars, beyond all the waiting-maids in Great Britain, the art of list'ning, madam, for your ladyship's service.

LUCINDA.
I shall soon know as much as you do. Leave me, leave me, Phillis, be gone. Here, here, I'll turn you out. My mother says I must not converse with my servants, though I must converse with no one else. *Exit* Phillis.
How unhappy are we who are born to great fortunes! No one looks at us with indifference or acts towards us on the foot of plain dealing. Yet, by all I have been heretofore offered to or treated for, I have been used with the most agreeable of all abuses, flattery; but now, by this phlegmatic fool I am used as nothing or a mere thing. He, forsooth, is too wise, too learned to have any regard to desires, and I know not what the learned oaf calls sentiments of love and passion. Here he comes with my mother. It's much if he looks at me. Or if he does, takes no more notice of me than of any other movable in the room. 205 210 215

Enter Mrs. Sealand *and* Mr. Cimberton.

MRS. SEALAND.
How do I admire this noble, this learned taste of yours and the worthy regard you have to our own ancient and honorable house in consulting a means to keep the blood as pure and as regularly descended as may be. 220

CIMBERTON.
Why, really, madam, the young women of this age are treated with discourses of such a tendency and their imaginations 225

214. I am] *O1–3*; I'm *D1.*

so bewildered in flesh and blood that a man of reason can't talk to be understood. They have no ideas of happiness but what are more gross than the gratification of hunger and thirst.

LUCINDA (*aside*).

With how much reflection he is a coxcomb! 230

CIMBERTON.

And in truth, madam, I have considered it as a most brutal custom that persons of the first character in the world should go as ordinarily and with as little shame to bed as to dinner with one another. They proceed to the propagation of the species as openly as to the preservation of the individual. 235

LUCINDA (*aside*).

She that willingly goes to bed to thee must have no shame, I'm sure.

MRS. SEALAND.

Oh, Cousin Cimberton! Cousin Cimberton! How abstracted, how refined is your sense of things! But, indeed, it is too true, there is nothing so ordinary as to say in the best governed 240 families, "My master and lady are gone to bed." One does not know but it might have been said of one's self.

Hiding her face with her fan.

CIMBERTON.

Lycurgus, madam, instituted otherwise. Among the Lacedemonians, the whole female world was pregnant, but none but the mothers themselves knew by whom. Their meetings 245 were secret and the amorous congress always by stealth, and no such professed doings between the sexes as are tolerated among us under the audacious word marriage.

MRS. SEALAND.

Oh, had I lived in those days and been a matron of Sparta, one might with less indecency have had ten children accord- 250 ing to that modest institution than one under the confusion of our modern, barefaced manner.

LUCINDA (*aside*).

And yet, poor woman, she has gone through the whole ceremony, and here I stand a melancholy proof of it.

---

243. *Lycurgus*] the lawgiver of Sparta or Lacedemonia.

MRS. SEALAND.

We will talk then of business. That girl walking about the room there is to be your wife. She has, I confess, no ideas, no sentiments that speak her born of a thinking mother. 255

CIMBERTON.

I have observed her. Her lively look, free air, and disengaged countenance speak her very—

LUCINDA.

Very what? 260

CIMBERTON.

If you please, madam, to set her a little that way.

MRS. SEALAND.

Lucinda, say nothing to him; you are not a match for him. When you are married, you may speak to such a husband when you're spoken to. But I am disposing of you above yourself every way. 265

CIMBERTON.

Madam, you cannot but observe the inconveniences I expose myself to in hopes that your ladyship will be the consort of my better part. As for the young woman, she is rather an impediment than a help to a man of letters and speculation. Madam, there is no reflection, no philosophy can at all times subdue the sensitive life, but the animal shall sometimes carry away the man. Ha! Ay, the vermilion of her lips. 270

LUCINDA.

Pray, don't talk of me thus.

CIMBERTON.

The pretty enough—pant of her bosom.

LUCINDA.

Sir! Madam, don't you hear him? 275

CIMBERTON.

Her forward chest.

LUCINDA.

Intolerable!

CIMBERTON.

High health.

---

268. *my better part*] *i.e.*, his intellect.
271. *sensitive*] sensuous.

LUCINDA.

The grave, easy impudence of him!

CIMBERTON.

Proud heart. 280

LUCINDA.

Stupid coxcomb!

CIMBERTON.

I say, madam, her impatience while we are looking at her throws out all attractions—her arms—her neck—what a spring in her step!

LUCINDA.

Don't you run me over thus, you strange unaccountable! 285

CIMBERTON.

What an elasticity in her veins and arteries!

LUCINDA.

I have no veins, no arteries.

MRS. SEALAND.

Oh, child, hear him, he talks finely, he's a scholar, he knows what you have.

CIMBERTON.

The speaking invitation of her shape, the gathering of her- 290 self up, and the indignation you see in the pretty little thing —now I am considering her on this occasion but as one that is to be pregnant.

LUCINDA (*aside*).

The familiar, learned, unseasonable puppy!

CIMBERTON.

And pregnant undoubtedly she will be yearly. I fear I shan't 295 for many years have discretion enough to give her one fallow season.

LUCINDA.

Monster! There's no bearing it. The hideous sot! There's no enduring it, to be thus surveyed like a steed at sale.

CIMBERTON.

At sale! She's very illiterate. But she's very well limbed too. 300 Turn her in. I see what she is.

MRS. SEALAND.

Go, you creature, I am ashamed of you.

Exit Lucinda *in a rage.*

---

301. *Turn her in*] drive her in (as one would say of *a steed at sale*).

CIMBERTON.

No harm done. You know, madam, the better sort of people, as I observed to you, treat by their lawyers of weddings (*adjusting himself at the glass*), and the woman in the bargain, 305 like the mansion-house in the sale of the estate, is thrown in, and what that is, whether good or bad, is not at all considered.

MRS. SEALAND.

I grant it, and therefore make no demand for her youth and beauty and every other accomplishment, as the common 310 world think 'em, because she is not polite.

CIMBERTON.

Madam, I know your exalted understanding, abstracted as it is from vulgar prejudices, will not be offended when I declare to you I marry to have an heir to my estate and not to beget a colony or a plantation. This young woman's beauty 315 and constitution will demand provision for a tenth child at least.

MRS. SEALAND (*aside*).

With all that wit and learning, how considerate! What an economist! —Sir, I cannot make her any other than she is, or say she is much better than the other young women of 320 this age or fit for much besides being a mother. But I have given directions for the marriage settlements, and Sir Geoffry Cimberton's counsel is to meet ours here, at this hour, concerning his joining in the deed, which, when executed, makes you capable of settling what is due to 325 Lucinda's fortune. Herself, as I told you, I say nothing of.

CIMBERTON.

No, no, no, indeed, madam, it is not usual, and I must depend upon my own reflection and philosophy not to overstock my family.

MRS. SEALAND.

I cannot help her, Cousin Cimberton, but she is, for aught I 330 see, as well as the daughter of anybody else.

CIMBERTON.

That is very true, madam.

314. to] *O1, D1*; *om. O2–3.*

---

311. *polite*] cultivated.
315. *plantation*] a company of settlers.

Enter a Servant, who whispers Mrs. Sealand.

MRS. SEALAND.

The lawyers are come, and now we are to hear what they have resolved as to the point whether it's necessary that Sir Geoffry should join in the settlement as being what they 335 call in the remainder. But, good cousin, you must have patience with 'em. These lawyers, I am told, are of a different kind. One is what they call a chamber-counsel, the other a pleader. The conveyancer is slow from an imperfection in his speech, and therefore shunned the bar, but extremely pas- 340 sionate and impatient of contradiction. The other is as warm as he but has a tongue so voluble and a head so conceited he will suffer nobody to speak but himself.

CIMBERTON.

You mean old Serjeant Target and Counsellor Bramble? I have heard of 'em. 345

MRS. SEALAND.

The same. Show in the gentlemen. *Exit* Servant.

Re-enter Servant, introducing Myrtle *and* Tom *disguised as Bramble and Target.*

MRS. SEALAND.

Gentlemen, this is the party concerned, Mr. Cimberton. And I hope you have considered of the matter.

TOM [*as* Target].

Yes, madam, we have agreed that it must be by indent—dent—dent—dent— 350

MYRTLE [*as* Bramble].

Yes, madam, Mr. Serjeant and myself have agreed, as he is pleased to inform you, that it must be an indenture tripartite, and tripartite let it be, for Sir Geoffry must needs be a party. Old Cimberton, in the year 1619, says in that ancient roll in Mr. Serjeant's hands, "as recourse thereto being had 355 —will more at large appear—"

349 ff. TOM. MYRTLE] *S.P.'s and S.D. read "Target" and "Bramble" in all editions.*

---

338. *chamber-counsel*] a lawyer who does not plead cases in court but gives opinions in private.

339. *pleader*] a trial lawyer.

TOM.

Yes, and by the deeds in your hands it appears that—

MYRTLE.

Mr. Serjeant, I beg of you to make no inferences upon what is in our custody, but speak to the titles in your own deeds. I shall not show that deed till my client is in town. 360

CIMBERTON.

You know best your own methods.

MRS. SEALAND.

The single question is whether the entail is such that my cousin Sir Geoffry is necessary in this affair?

MYRTLE.

Yes, as to the lordship of Tretriplet but not as to the messuage of Grimgribber. 365

TOM.

I say that Gr—gr—that Gr—gr—Grimgribber, Grimgribber is in us. That is to say the remainder thereof, as well as that of Tr—tr—Triplet.

MYRTLE.

You go upon the deed of Sir Ralph, made in the middle of the last century, precedent to that in which old Cimberton 370 made over the remainder and made it pass to the heirs general, by which your client comes in; and I question whether the remainder even of Tretriplet is in him. But we are willing to waive that and give him a valuable consideration. But we shall not purchase what is in us forever, as Grimgribber is, 375 at the rate as we guard against the contingent of Mr. Cimberton having no son. Then we know Sir Geoffry is the first of the collateral male line in this family. Yet—

TOM.

Sir, Gr—gr—ber is—

MYRTLE.

I apprehend you very well, and your argument might be of 380 force, and we would be inclined to hear that in all its parts. But sir, I see very plainly what you are going into. I tell you,

382. plainly] *O1(c)*, *D1*; plain *O1(u)*, *O2–3*.

364–365. *messuage*] the house, outbuildings, and adjoining land.

366. *Grimgribber*] This term, invented by Steele, was later used to mean legal gibberish.

it is as probable a contingent that Sir Geoffry may die before Mr. Cimberton as that he may outlive him.

TOM.

Sir, we are not ripe for that yet, but I must say— 385

MYRTLE.

Sir, I allow you the whole extent of that argument, but that will go no farther than as to the claimants under old Cimberton. I am of opinion that according to the instruction of Sir Ralph, he could not dock the entail and then create a new estate for the heirs general. 390

TOM.

Sir, I have not patience to be told that, when Gr—gr—ber—

MYRTLE.

I will allow it you, Mr. Serjeant, but there must be the word "heirs forever" to make such an estate as you pretend.

CIMBERTON.

I must be impartial, though you are counsel for my side of the question. Were it not that you are so good as to allow 395 him what he has not said, I should think it very hard you should answer him without hearing him. But gentlemen, I believe you have both considered this matter and are firm in your different opinions. 'Twere better therefore you proceeded according to the particular sense of each of you and 400 gave your thoughts distinctly in writing. And do you see, sirs, pray let me have a copy of what you say, in English.

MYRTLE.

Why, what is all we have been saying? In English! Oh! But I forgot myself, you're a wit. But however, to please you, sir, you shall have it in as plain terms as the law will admit of. 405

CIMBERTON.

But I would have it, sir, without delay.

MYRTLE.

That, sir, the law will not admit of. The courts are sitting at Westminster, and I am this moment obliged to be at every one of them, and 'twould be wrong if I should not be in the Hall to attend one of 'em at least; the rest would take it ill 410 else. Therefore, I must leave what I have said to Mr. Ser-

---

389. *dock the entail*] change the legal succession to the estate.
409–410. *the Hall*] Westminster Hall, where trials were held.

jeant's consideration, and I will digest his arguments on my part, and you shall hear from me again, sir. *Exit* Myrtle.

TOM.

Agreed, agreed.

CIMBERTON.

Mr. Bramble is very quick. He parted a little abruptly. 415

TOM.

He could not bear my argument; I pinched him to the quick about that Gr—gr—ber.

MRS. SEALAND.

I saw that, for he durst not so much as hear you—I shall send to you, Mr. Serjeant, as soon as Sir Geoffry comes to town, and then I hope all may be adjusted. 420

TOM.

I shall be at my chambers at my usual hours. *Exit.*

CIMBERTON.

Madam, if you please, I'll now attend you to the tea table, where I shall hear from your ladyship reason and good sense, after all this law and gibberish.

MRS. SEALAND.

'Tis a wonderful thing, sir, that men of professions do not 425 study to talk the substance of what they have to say in the language of the rest of the world. Sure, they'd find their account in it.

CIMBERTON.

They might, perhaps, madam, with people of your good sense; but, with the generality 'twould never do. The vulgar 430 would have no respect for truth and knowledge if they were exposed to naked view.

Truth is too simple, of all art bereaved:
Since the world will—why, let it be deceived. *Exeunt.*

---

425. *wonderful*] astonishing.
428. *account*] advantage, profit.

ACT IV

[IV.i]

Scene, Bevil Junior's lodgings. Bevil Junior *with a letter in his hand, followed by* Tom.

TOM.

Upon my life, sir, I know nothing of the matter; I never opened my lips to Mr. Myrtle about anything of your honor's letter to Madam Lucinda.

BEVIL JUNIOR [*aside*].

What's the fool in such a fright for? —I don't suppose you did. What I would know is whether Mr. Myrtle showed any suspicion or asked you any questions to lead you to say casually that you had carried any such letter for me this morning. 5

TOM.

Why, sir, if he did ask me any questions, how could I help it?

BEVIL JUNIOR.

I don't say you could, oaf! I am not questioning you, but him. What did he say to you? 10

TOM.

Why, sir, when I came to his chambers to be dressed for the lawyer's part your honor was pleased to put me upon, he asked me if I had been at Mr. Sealand's this morning. So I told him, sir, I often went thither, because, sir, if I had not said that, he might have thought there was something more in my going now than at another time. 15

BEVIL JUNIOR.

Very well. (*Aside.*) The fellow's caution, I find, has given him this jealousy. —Did he ask you no other questions?

TOM.

Yes sir, now I remember, as we came away in the hackney coach from Mr. Sealand's, "Tom," says he, "as I came in to your master this morning, he bad you go for an answer to a letter he had sent. Pray did you bring him any?" says he. "Ah!" says I, "Sir, your honor is pleased to joke with me; you have a mind to know whether I can keep a secret or no?" 20

BEVIL JUNIOR.

And so, by showing him you could, you told him you had one? 25

TOM (*confused*).

Sir—

BEVIL JUNIOR [*aside*].

What mean actions does jealousy make a man stoop to! How poorly has he used art with a servant to make him betray his master!—Well! And when did he give you this letter for me? 30

TOM.

Sir, he writ it before he pulled off his lawyer's gown at his own chambers.

BEVIL JUNIOR.

Very well; and what did he say when you brought him my answer to it?

TOM.

He looked a little out of humor, sir, and said it was very well. 35

BEVIL JUNIOR.

I knew he would be grave upon't. Wait without.

TOM [*aside*].

Humh! 'Gad, I don't like this; I am afraid we are all in the wrong box here. *Exit* Tom.

BEVIL JUNIOR.

I put on a serenity while my fellow was present, but I have never been more thoroughly disturbed. This hot man! To 40 write me a challenge on supposed artificial dealing when I professed myself his friend! I can live contented without glory, but I cannot suffer shame. What's to be done? But first, let me consider Lucinda's letter again. *Reads.*

"SIR, 45

I hope it is consistent with the laws a woman ought to impose upon herself to acknowledge that your manner of declining a treaty of marriage in our family and desiring the refusal may come from hence has something more engaging in it than the courtship of him, who, I fear, will fall to my lot 50 except your friend exerts himself for our common safety and happiness. I have reasons for desiring Mr. Myrtle may not

29. his] *O1(c), O2–3, D1*; his own *O1(u)*.

49. hence] *O1(c), O2–3*; me *O1(u), D1*.

---

29. *art*] artifice.

37–38. *in . . . box*] out of place.

know of this letter till hereafter and am your most obliged humble servant,

LUCINDA SEALAND." 55

Well, but the postscript. *Reads.*

"I won't, upon second thoughts, hide anything from you. But my reason for concealing this is that Mr. Myrtle has a jealousy in his temper which gives me some terrors. But my esteem for him inclines me to hope that only an ill effect 60 which sometimes accompanies a tender love, and what may be cured by a careful and unblamable conduct."

Thus has this lady made me her friend and confident and put herself in a kind under my protection. I cannot tell him immediately the purport of her letter except I could cure 65 him of the violent and untractable passion of jealousy and so serve him and her by disobeying her in the article of secrecy more than I should by complying with her directions. But then this dueling, which custom has imposed upon every man who would live with reputation and honor in the world— 70 how must I preserve myself from imputations there? He'll, forsooth, call it, or think it fear if I explain without fighting. But his letter—I'll read it again.

[*Reads.*]

"SIR,

You have used me basely in corresponding and carrying 75 on a treaty where you told me you were indifferent. I have changed my sword since I saw you, which advertisement I thought proper to send you against the next meeting between you and the injured

CHARLES MYRTLE." 80

Enter Tom.

TOM.

Mr. Myrtle, sir. Would your honor please to see him?

BEVIL JUNIOR.

Why you stupid creature! Let Mr. Myrtle wait at my lodgings! Show him up. *Exit* Tom.

Well, I am resolved upon my carriage to him. He is in love, and in every circumstance of life a little distrustful, which I 85 must allow for. But here he is.

Enter Tom *introducing* Myrtle.

Sir, I am extremely obliged to you for this honor. [*To* Tom.] But, sir, you, with your very discerning face, leave the room. *Exit* Tom.
Well, Mr. Myrtle, your commands with me? 90

MYRTLE.
The time, the place, our long acquaintance, and many other circumstances which affect me on this occasion oblige me, without farther ceremony or conference, to desire you would not only, as you already have, acknowledge the receipt of my letter, but also comply with the request in it. I 95 must have farther notice taken of my message than these half lines, "I have yours—I shall be at home—"

BEVIL JUNIOR.
Sir, I own I have received a letter from you in a very unusual style. But as I design everything in this matter shall be your own action, your own seeking, I shall understand 100 nothing but what you are pleased to confirm face to face, and I have already forgot the contents of your epistle.

MYRTLE.
This cool manner is very agreeable to the abuse you have already made of my simplicity and frankness, and I see your moderation tends to your own advantage and not mine, to 105 your own safety, not consideration of your friend.

BEVIL JUNIOR.
My own safety, Mr. Myrtle!

MYRTLE.
Your own safety, Mr. Bevil.

BEVIL JUNIOR.
Look you, Mr. Myrtle, there's no disguising that I understand what you would be at, but, sir, you know, I have of- 110 ten dared to disapprove of the decisions a tyrant custom has introduced to the breach of all laws, both divine and human.

MYRTLE.
Mr. Bevil, Mr. Bevil, it would be a good first principle in those who have so tender a conscience that way to have as 115 much abhorrence of doing injuries as—

BEVIL JUNIOR.

As what?

MYRTLE.

As fear of answering for 'em.

BEVIL JUNIOR.

As fear of answering for 'em! But that apprehension is just or blamable according to the object of that fear. I have often 120 told you in confidence of heart I abhorred the daring to offend the Author of Life and rushing into His presence—I say, by the very same act to commit the crime against him and immediately to urge on to his tribunal.

MYRTLE.

Mr. Bevil, I must tell you, this coolness, this gravity, this 125 show of conscience shall never cheat me of my mistress. You have, indeed, the best excuse for life, the hopes of possessing Lucinda. But consider, sir, I have as much reason to be weary of it if I am to lose her. And my first attempt to recover her shall be to let her see the dauntless man who is to be her 130 guardian and protector.

BEVIL JUNIOR.

Sir, show me but the least glimpse of argument that I am authorized by my own hand to vindicate any lawless insult of this nature, and I will show thee—to chastise thee—hardly deserves the name of courage—slight, inconsiderate 135 man! There is, Mr. Myrtle, no such terror in quick anger; and you shall, you know not why, be cool, as you have, you know not why, been warm.

MYRTLE.

Is the woman one loves so little an occasion of anger? You, perhaps, who know not what it is to love, who have your 140 ready, your commodious, your foreign trinket for your loose hours, and from your fortune, your specious outward carriage, and other lucky circumstances, as easy a way to the possession of a woman of honor, you know nothing of what it is to be alarmed, to be distracted with anxiety and terror of 145 losing more than life. Your marriage, happy man, goes on like common business, and in the interim you have your rambling captive, your Indian princess for your soft moments of dalliance, your convenient, your ready Indiana.

BEVIL JUNIOR.

You have touched me beyond the patience of a man, and 150
I'm excusable, in the guard of innocence—or from the infirmity of human nature which can bear no more—to accept your invitation and observe your letter. Sir, I'll attend you.

Enter Tom.

TOM.

Did you call, sir? I thought you did; I heard you speak aloud. 155

BEVIL JUNIOR.

Yes, go call a coach.

TOM.

Sir—master—Mr. Myrtle—friends—gentlemen—what d'ye mean? I am but a servant, or—

BEVIL JUNIOR.

Call a coach. *Exit* Tom.

A long pause, walking sullenly by each other.

(*Aside.*) Shall I, though provoked to the uttermost, re- 160
cover myself at the entrance of a third person, and that my servant too, and not have respect enough to all I have ever been receiving from infancy, the obligation to the best of fathers, to an unhappy virgin too, whose life depends on mine? *Shutting the door.* 165
(*To* Myrtle.) I have, thank Heaven, had time to recollect myself, and shall not, for fear of what such a rash man as you think of me, keep longer unexplained the false appearances under which your infirmity of temper makes you suffer, when, perhaps, too much regard to a false point of honor makes me 170
prolong that suffering.

MYRTLE.

I am sure Mr. Bevil cannot doubt but I had rather have satisfaction from his innocence than his sword.

BEVIL JUNIOR.

Why then would you ask it first that way?

MYRTLE.

Consider, you kept your temper yourself no longer than till 175
I spoke to the disadvantage of her you loved.

BEVIL JUNIOR.

True. But let me tell you, I have saved you from the most exquisite distress even though you had succeeded in the dispute. I know you so well that I am sure to have found this letter about a man you had killed would have been worse 180 than death to yourself. Read it. [*Aside.*] When he is thoroughly mortified and shame has got the better of jealousy, when he has seen himself throughly, he will deserve to be assisted towards obtaining Lucinda.

MYRTLE [*aside*].

With what a superiority has he turned the injury on me as 185 the aggressor! I begin to fear I have been too far transported. "A treaty in our family!" Is not that saying too much? I shall relapse. But, I find, on the postscript, "something like jealousy"—with what face can I see my benefactor, my advocate, whom I have treated like a betrayer? —Oh! Bevil, 190 with what words shall I—

BEVIL JUNIOR.

There needs none; to convince is much more than to conquer.

MYRTLE.

But can you—

BEVIL JUNIOR.

You have o'erpaid the inquietude you gave me in the change 195 I see in you towards me. Alas, what machines are we! Thy face is altered to that of another man, to that of my companion, my friend.

MYRTLE.

That I could be such a precipitant wretch!

BEVIL JUNIOR.

Pray, no more. 200

MYRTLE.

Let me reflect how many friends have died by the hands of friends for want of temper. And you must give me leave to say again and again how much I am beholden to that superior spirit you have subdued me with. What had become of one of us, or perhaps both, had you been as weak as I was and 205 as incapable of reason?

---

183. *throughly*] thoroughly.

BEVIL JUNIOR.

I congratulate to us both the escape from ourselves and hope the memory of it will make us dearer friends than ever.

MYRTLE.

Dear Bevil, your friendly conduct has convinced me that there is nothing manly but what is conducted by reason and 210 agreeable to the practice of virtue and justice. And yet, how many have been sacrificed to that idol, the unreasonable opinion of men! Nay, they are so ridiculous in it that they often use their swords against each other with dissembled anger and real fear. 215

Betrayed by honor, and compelled by shame,
They hazard being, to preserve a name:
Nor dare inquire into the dread mistake,
Till plunged in sad eternity they wake.

Exeunt.

[IV.ii]

Scene, St. James's Park. Enter Sir John Bevil *and* Mr. Sealand.

SIR JOHN BEVIL.

Give me leave, however, Mr. Sealand, as we are upon a treaty for uniting our families, to mention only the business of an ancient house. Genealogy and descent are to be of some consideration in an affair of this sort—

MR. SEALAND.

Genealogy and descent! Sir, there has been in our family a 5 very large one. There was Galfrid, the father of Edward, the father of Ptolemy, the father of Crassus, the father of Earl Richard, the father of Henry the Marquis, the father of Duke John—

SIR JOHN BEVIL.

What, do you rave, Mr. Sealand? All these great names in 10 your family?

MR. SEALAND.

These? Yes sir, I have heard my father name 'em all, and more.

SIR JOHN BEVIL.

Ay, sir? And did he say they were all in your family?

MR. SEALAND.

Yes sir, he kept 'em all, he was the greatest cocker in England. He said Duke John won him many battles and never lost one. 15

SIR JOHN BEVIL.

Oh sir, your servant, you are laughing at my laying any stress upon descent. But I must tell you, sir, I never knew anyone but he that wanted that advantage, turn it into ridicule. 20

MR. SEALAND.

And I never knew anyone who had many better advantages put that into his account. But, Sir John, value yourself as you please upon your ancient house, I am to talk freely of everything you are pleased to put into your bill of rates on this occasion. Yet, sir, I have made no objections to your son's family. 'Tis his morals that I doubt. 25

SIR JOHN BEVIL.

Sir, I can't help saying that what might injure a citizen's credit may be no stain to a gentleman's honor.

MR. SEALAND.

Sir John, the honor of a gentleman is liable to be tainted by as small a matter as the credit of a trader. We are talking of a marriage, and in such a case, the father of a young woman will not think it an addition to the honor or credit of her lover—that he is a keeper— 30

SIR JOHN BEVIL.

Mr. Sealand, don't take upon you to spoil my son's marriage with any woman else. 35

MR. SEALAND.

Sir John, let him apply to any woman else and have as many mistresses as he pleases—

SIR JOHN BEVIL.

My son, sir, is a discreet and sober gentleman—

MR. SEALAND.

Sir, I never saw a man that wenched soberly and discreetly that ever left it off. The decency observed in the practice hides even from the sinner the iniquity of it. They pursue it, not that their appetites hurry 'em away, but, I warrant you, because 'tis their opinion they may do it. 40

---

15. *cocker*] breeder of fighting cocks.

SIR JOHN BEVIL.

Were what you suspect a truth, do you design to keep your daughter a virgin till you find a man unblemished that way? 45

MR. SEALAND.

Sir, as much a cit as you take me for, I know the town and the world. And give me leave to say that we merchants are a species of gentry that have grown into the world this last century, and are as honorable, and almost as useful, as you landed folks that have always thought yourselves so much 50 above us. For your trading, forsooth, is extended no farther than a load of hay or a fat ox. You are pleasant people, indeed, because you are generally bred up to be lazy; therefore, I warrant you, industry is dishonorable.

SIR JOHN BEVIL.

Be not offended, sir; let us go back to our point. 55

MR. SEALAND.

Oh, not at all offended—but I don't love to leave any part of the account unclosed. Look you, Sir John, comparisons are odious, and more particularly so on occasions of this kind when we are projecting races that are to be made out of both sides of the comparisons. 60

SIR JOHN BEVIL.

But my son, sir, is, in the eye of the world, a gentleman of merit.

MR. SEALAND.

I own to you, I think him so. But, Sir John, I am a man exercised and experienced in chances and disasters. I lost, in my earlier years, a very fine wife, and with her a poor little 65 infant; that makes me, perhaps, over-cautious to preserve the second bounty of Providence to me, and be as careful as I can of this child. You'll pardon me, my poor girl, sir, is as valuable to me as your boasted son to you.

SIR JOHN BEVIL.

Why, that's one very good reason, Mr. Sealand, why I wish 70 my son had her.

MR. SEALAND.

There is nothing but this strange lady here, this *incognita*,

---

46. *cit*] a contemptuous term for middle-class tradesmen.

that can be objected to him. Here and there a man falls in love with an artful creature and gives up all the motives of life to that one passion. 75

SIR JOHN BEVIL.

A man of my son's understanding cannot be supposed to be one of them.

MR. SEALAND.

Very wise men have been so enslaved; and when a man marries with one of them upon his hands, whether moved from the demand of the world or slighter reasons, such a husband 80 soils with his wife for a month perhaps, then good b'w'y', madam—the show's over. Ah! John Dryden points out such a husband to a hair where he says,

"And while abroad so prodigal the dolt is,
Poor spouse at home as ragged as a colt is." 85

Now in plain terms, sir, I shall not care to have my poor girl turned a-grazing, and that must be the case when—

SIR JOHN BEVIL.

But pray consider, sir, my son—

MR. SEALAND.

Look you, sir, I'll make the matter short. This unknown lady, as I told you, is all the objection I have to him. But, 90 one way or other, he is, or has been, certainly engaged to her. I am therefore resolved this very afternoon to visit her. Now from her behavior or appearance, I shall soon be let into what I may fear or hope for.

SIR JOHN BEVIL.

Sir, I am very confident there can be nothing inquired into, 95 relating to my son, that will not, upon being understood, turn to his advantage.

MR. SEALAND.

I hope that as sincerely as you believe it. Sir John Bevil, when I am satisfied in this great point, if your son's conduct answers the character you give him, I shall wish your alliance 100

---

81. *soils*] cohabits.

84–85. "*And . . . is.*"] quoted from Dryden's epilogue to Vanbrugh's *The Pilgrim* (1700), ll. 41–42, but "For" is changed to "And". A similar couplet in his prologue to Southerne's *The Disappointment* (1684). ll. 55–56, differs in the first line, "But while abroad so liberal the dolt is".

more than that of any gentleman in Great Britain, and so your servant. *Exit.*

SIR JOHN BEVIL.

He is gone in a way but barely civil. But his great wealth and the merit of his only child, the heiress of it, are not to be lost for a little peevishness. 105

Enter Humphrey.

Oh, Humphrey, you are come in a seasonable minute. I want to talk to thee and to tell thee that my head and heart are on the rack about my son.

HUMPHREY.

Sir, you may trust his discretion; I am sure you may.

SIR JOHN BEVIL.

Why, I do believe I may, and yet I'm in a thousand fears 110 when I lay this vast wealth before me. When I consider his prepossessions, either generous to a folly in an honorable love or abandoned past redemption in a vicious one, and from the one or the other, his insensibility to the fairest prospect towards doubling our estate, a father, who knows how 115 useful wealth is, and how necessary, even to those who despise it, I say a father, Humphrey, a father cannot bear it.

HUMPHREY.

Be not transported, sir; you will grow incapable of taking any resolution in your perplexity.

SIR JOHN BEVIL.

Yet, as angry as I am with him, I would not have him sur- 120 prised in anything. This mercantile rough man may go grossly into the examination of this matter and talk to the gentlewoman so as to—

HUMPHREY.

No, I hope, not in an abrupt manner.

SIR JOHN BEVIL.

No, I hope not. Why, dost thou know anything of her, or of 125 him, or of anything of it, or all of it?

HUMPHREY.

My dear master, I know so much; that I told him this very day you had reason to be secretly out of humor about her.

SIR JOHN BEVIL.

Did you go so far? Well, what said he to that?

HUMPHREY.

His words were, looking upon me steadfastly, "Humphrey," 130
says he, "that woman is a woman of honor."

SIR JOHN BEVIL.

How! Do you think he is married to her or designs to marry
her?

HUMPHREY.

I can say nothing to the latter. But he says he can marry no
one without your consent while you are living. 135

SIR JOHN BEVIL.

If he said so much, I know he scorns to break his word with
me.

HUMPHREY.

I am sure of that.

SIR JOHN BEVIL.

You are sure of that—well, that's some comfort. Then I
have nothing to do but to see the bottom of this matter 140
during this present ruffle—oh, Humphrey—

HUMPHREY.

You are not ill, I hope, sir.

SIR JOHN BEVIL.

Yes, a man is very ill that's in a very ill humor. To be a father
is to be in care for one whom you oftener disoblige than
please by that very care. Oh, that sons could know the duty 145
to a father before they themselves are fathers! But, perhaps,
you'll say now that I am one of the happiest fathers in the
world; but, I assure you, that of the very happiest is not a
condition to be envied.

HUMPHREY.

Sir, your pain arises not from the thing itself but your par- 150
ticular sense of it—you are overfond, nay, give me leave to
say, you are unjustly apprehensive from your fondness. My
master Bevil never disobliged you, and he will, I know he
will, do everything you ought to expect.

SIR JOHN BEVIL.

He won't take all this money with this girl. For aught I know, 155
he will, forsooth, have so much moderation as to think he
ought not to force his liking for any consideration.

---

141. *ruffle*] commotion.

HUMPHREY.

He is to marry her, not you; he is to live with her, not you, sir.

SIR JOHN BEVIL.

I know not what to think. But I know nothing can be more miserable than to be in this doubt. Follow me; I must come to some resolution. 160 *Exeunt.*

[IV.iii]

Scene, Bevil Junior's lodgings. Enter Tom *and* Phillis.

TOM.

Well, madam, if you must speak with Mr. Myrtle, you shall. He is now with my master in the library.

PHILLIS.

But you must leave me alone with him, for he can't make me a present, nor I so handsomely take anything from him before you; it would not be decent. 5

TOM.

It will be very decent, indeed, for me to retire and leave my mistress with another man.

PHILLIS.

He is a gentleman and will treat one properly.

TOM.

I believe so. But, however, I won't be far off and therefore will venture to trust you. I'll call him to you. *Exit* Tom. 10

PHILLIS.

What a deal of pother and sputter here is between my mistress and Mr. Myrtle from mere punctilio! I could any hour of the day get her to her lover and would do it, but she, forsooth, will allow no plot to get him. But if he can come to her, I know she would be glad of it. I must therefore do her an acceptable violence and surprise her into his arms. I am sure I go by the best rule imaginable—if she were my maid, I should think her the best servant in the world for doing so by me. 15

Enter Myrtle *and* Tom.

Oh sir, you and Mr. Bevil are fine gentlemen to let a lady 20

---

11. *pother*] fuss.

remain under such difficulties as my poor mistress, and no attempt to set her at liberty or release her from the danger of being instantly married to Cimberton.

MYRTLE.

Tom has been telling. But what is to be done?

PHILLIS.

What is to be done—when a man can't come at his mistress! 25
Why, can't you fire our house or the next house to us, to make us run out and you take us?

MYRTLE.

How, Mrs. Phillis—

PHILLIS.

Ay, let me see that rogue [*indicating* Tom] deny to fire a house, make a riot, or any other little thing, when there were 30
no other way to come at me.

TOM.

I am obliged to you, madam.

PHILLIS.

Why, don't we hear every day of people's hanging themselves for love, and won't they venture the hazard of being hanged for love? Oh! Were I a man— 35

MYRTLE.

What manly thing would you have me undertake, according to your ladyship's notion of a man?

PHILLIS.

Only be at once what, one time or other, you may be, and wish to be, or must be.

MYRTLE.

Dear girl, talk plainly to me, and consider, I, in my con- 40
dition, can't be in very good humor. You say, to be at once what I must be.

PHILLIS.

Ay, ay, I mean no more than to be an old man. I saw you do it very well at the masquerade. In a word, old Sir Geoffry Cimberton is every hour expected in town to join in the deeds 45
and settlements for marrying Mr. Cimberton. He is half blind, half lame, half deaf, half dumb; though as to his passions and desires, he is as warm and ridiculous as when in the heat of youth—

35. I a] *O1, O3, D1*; a I *O2.*

TOM.

Come to the business, and don't keep the gentleman in suspense for the pleasure of being courted, as you serve me. 50

PHILLIS.

I saw you at the masquerade act such a one to perfection. Go and put on that very habit, and come to our house as Sir Geoffry. There is not one there but myself knows his person. I was born in the parish where he is lord of the manor. I have seen him often and often at church in the country. Do not hesitate, but come thither. They will think you bring a certain security against Mr. Myrtle, and you bring Mr. Myrtle. Leave the rest to me, I leave this with you, and expect— They don't, I told you, know you; they think you out of town, which you had as good be forever, if you lose this opportunity. I must be gone; I know I am wanted at home. 55 60

MYRTLE.

My dear Phillis!

Catches and kisses her, and gives her money.

PHILLIS.

O fie! My kisses are not my own; you have committed violence, but I'll carry 'em to the right owner. 65

Tom *kisses her.*

(*To* Tom.) Come, see me downstairs, and leave the lover to think of his last game for the prize. *Exeunt* Tom *and* Phillis.

MYRTLE.

I think I will instantly attempt this wild expedient. The extravagance of it will make me less suspected, and it will give me opportunity to assert my own right to Lucinda, without whom I cannot live. But I am so mortified at this conduct of mine towards poor Bevil. He must think meanly of me. I know not how to reassume myself and be in spirit enough for such an adventure as this. Yet I must attempt it, if it be only to be near Lucinda under her present perplexities. And sure— 70 75

The next delight to transport with the fair
Is to relieve her in her hours of care. *Exit.*

---

74. *reassume myself*] become my normal self again.

ACT V

[V.i]

Scene, Sealand's house. Enter Phillis *with lights before* Myrtle, *disguised like old Sir Geoffry, supported by* Mrs. Sealand, Lucinda, *and* Cimberton.

MRS. SEALAND.

Now I have seen you thus far, Sir Geoffry, will you excuse me a moment while I give my necessary orders for your accommodation? *Exit* Mrs. Sealand.

MYRTLE.

I have not seen you, Cousin Cimberton, since you were ten years old, and as it is incumbent on you to keep up our name and family, I shall upon very reasonable terms join with you in a settlement to that purpose. Though I must tell you, cousin, this is the first merchant that has married into our house. 5

LUCINDA (*aside*).

Deuce on 'em! Am I a merchant because my father is? 10

MYRTLE.

But is he directly a trader at this time?

CIMBERTON.

There's no hiding the disgrace, sir; he trades to all parts of the world.

MYRTLE.

We never had one of our family before who descended from persons that did anything. 15

CIMBERTON.

Sir, since it is a girl that they have, I am, for the honor of my family, willing to take it in again and to sink her into our name and no harm done.

MYRTLE.

'Tis prudently and generously resolved. Is this the young thing? 20

CIMBERTON.

Yes sir.

PHILLIS [*apart to* Lucinda].

Good madam, don't be out of humor but let them run to the utmost of their extravagance. Hear them out.

MYRTLE.

Can't I see her nearer? My eyes are but weak.

PHILLIS [*apart to* Lucinda].

Besides, I am sure the uncle has something worth your notice, I'll take care to get off the young one and leave you to observe what may be wrought out of the old one for your good. *Exit.* 25

CIMBERTON.

Madam, this old gentleman, your great-uncle, desires to be introduced to you and to see you nearer. Approach, sir. 30

MYRTLE.

By your leave, young lady— (*Puts on spectacles.*) Cousin Cimberton! She has exactly that sort of neck and bosom for which my sister Gertrude was so much admired in the year sixty-one before the French dresses first discovered anything in women below the chin. 35

LUCINDA (*aside*).

What a very odd situation am I in! Though I cannot but be diverted at the extravagance of their humors, equally unsuitable to their age—chin, quotha—I don't believe my passionate lover there knows whether I have one or not. Ha! Ha! 40

MYRTLE.

Madam. I would not willingly offend, but I have a better glass— *Pulls out a large one.*

Enter Phillis *to* Cimberton.

PHILLIS.

Sir, my lady desires to show the apartment to you that she intends for Sir Geoffry.

CIMBERTON.

Well sir, by that time you have sufficiently gazed and sunned yourself in the beauties of my spouse there, I will wait on you again. *Exit* Cimberton *and* Phillis. 45

MYRTLE.

Were it not, madam, that I might be troublesome, there is

43. Sir] *O2–3, D1*; *om. O1.*

---

38. *quotha*] an expression of contempt, originally meaning "said he."
42. *glass*] optical instrument.

something of importance, though we are alone, which I would say more safe from being heard. 50

LUCINDA [*aside*].

There is something in this old fellow, methinks, that raises my curiosity.

MYRTLE.

To be free, madam, I as heartily contemn this kinsman of mine as you do and am sorry to see so much beauty and merit devoted by your parents to so insensible a possessor. 55

LUCINDA [*aside*].

Surprising!—I hope then, sir, you will not contribute to the wrong you are so generous as to pity, whatever may be the interest of your family.

MYRTLE.

This hand of mine shall never be employed to sign anything against your good and happiness. 60

LUCINDA.

I am sorry, sir, it is not in my power to make you proper acknowledgements, but there is a gentleman in the world whose gratitude will, I am sure, be worthy of the favor.

MYRTLE.

All the thanks I desire, madam, are in your power to give.

LUCINDA.

Name them, and command them. 65

MYRTLE.

Only, madam, that the first time you are alone with your lover, you will, with open arms, receive him.

LUCINDA.

As willingly as his heart could wish it.

MYRTLE.

Thus then he claims your promise! Oh, Lucinda!

LUCINDA.

Oh! A cheat! A cheat! A cheat! 70

MYRTLE.

Hush! 'Tis I, 'tis I, your lover, Myrtle himself, madam.

LUCINDA.

Oh bless me! What a rashness and folly to surprise me so—But hush—my mother—

Enter Mrs. Sealand, Cimberton, *and* Phillis.

MRS. SEALAND.

How now! What's the matter?

LUCINDA.

Oh madam! As soon as you left the room, my uncle fell into a sudden fit, and—and—so I cried out for help, to support him, and conduct him to his chamber. 75

MRS. SEALAND.

That was kindly done! Alas! Sir, how do you find yourself?

MYRTLE.

Never was taken in so odd a way in my life. Pray lead me! Oh! I was talking here—pray carry me—to my Cousin Cimberton's young lady— 80

MRS. SEALAND (*aside*).

My Cousin Cimberton's young lady! How zealous he is, even in his extremity, for the match! A right Cimberton!

Cimberton *and* Lucinda *lead him, as one in pain, etc.*

CIMBERTON.

Pox! Uncle, you will pull my ear off.

LUCINDA.

Pray uncle! You will squeeze me to death. 85

MRS. SEALAND.

No matter, no matter, he knows not what he does. Come, sir, shall I help you out?

MYRTLE.

By no means; I'll trouble nobody but my young cousins here. *They lead him off.*

PHILLIS.

But pray, madam, does your ladyship intend that Mr. Cimberton shall really marry my young mistress at last? I don't think he likes her. 90

MRS. SEALAND.

That's not material! Men of his speculation are above desires. But be it as it may, now I have given old Sir Geoffry the trouble of coming up to sign and seal, with what countenance can I be off? 95

---

83. *right*] true.
93. *speculation*] intelligence, vision.

PHILLIS.

As well as with twenty others, madam. It is the glory and honor of a great fortune to live in continual treaties and still to break off. It looks great, madam.

MRS. SEALAND.

True, Phillis. Yet to return our blood again into the Cimbertons is an honor not to be rejected. But were not you saying that Sir John Bevil's creature Humphrey has been with Mr. Sealand? 100

PHILLIS.

Yes, madam: I overheard them agree that Mr. Sealand should go himself and visit this unknown lady that Mr. Bevil is so great with; and if he found nothing there to fright him, that Mr. Bevil should still marry my young mistress. 105

MRS. SEALAND.

How! Nay then, he shall find she is my daughter as well as his: I'll follow him this instant and take the whole family along with me. The disputed power of disposing of my own daughter shall be at an end this very night. I'll live no longer in anxiety for a little hussy that hurts my appearance where-ever I carry her and for whose sake I seem to be not at all regarded, and that in the best of my days. 110

PHILLIS.

Indeed, madam, if she were married, your ladyship might very well be taken for Mr. Sealand's daughter. 115

MRS. SEALAND.

Nay, when the chit has not been with me, I have heard the men say as much. I'll no longer cut off the greatest pleasure of a woman's life, the shining in assemblies, by her forward anticipation of the respect that's due to her superior—she shall down to Cimberton-Hall—she shall—she shall. 120

PHILLIS.

I hope, madam, I shall stay with your ladyship.

MRS. SEALAND.

Thou shalt, Phillis, and I'll place thee then more about me. But order chairs immediately; I'll be gone this minute.

Exeunt.

113. not] *Dub.*; *om. O1–3, D1.*

[V.ii] *Scene, Charing Cross. Enter* Mr. Sealand *and* Humphrey.

MR. SEALAND.

I am very glad, Mr. Humphrey, that you agree with me that it is for our common good I should look thoroughly into this matter.

HUMPHREY.

I am indeed of that opinion, for there is no artifice, nothing concealed in our family which ought in justice to be known. 5
I need not desire you, sir, to treat the lady with care and respect.

MR. SEALAND.

Master Humphrey, I shall not be rude, though I design to be a little abrupt and come into the matter at once to see how she will bear upon a surprise. 10

HUMPHREY.

That's the door, sir, I wish you success.

While Humphrey *speaks,* Mr. Sealand *consults his table-book.*

[*Aside.*] I am less concerned what happens there because I hear Mr. Myrtle is well-lodged as old Sir Geoffry, so I am willing to let this gentleman employ himself here to give them time at home, for I am sure 'tis necessary for the quiet 15
of our family Lucinda were disposed of out of it, since Mr. Bevil's inclination is so much otherwise engaged. *Exit.*

MR. SEALAND.

I think this is the door. *Knocks.*
I'll carry this matter with an air of authority to inquire, though I make an errand to begin discourse. 20

Knocks again, and enter a footboy [Daniel].

So young man! Is your lady within?

DANIEL.

Alack, sir! I am but a country boy—I dan't know whether she is or noa. But an you'll stay a bit, I'll goa and ask the gentlewoman that's with her.

22 ff. DANIEL] *S.P.'s and S.D.'s read* BOY *in all editions.*

11.1. *table-book*] pocket notebook.
20. *make*] invent.

MR. SEALAND.

Why, sirrah, though you are a country boy, you can see, can't you? You know whether she is at home when you see her, don't you? 25

DANIEL.

Nay, nay, I'm not such a country lad neither, master, to think she's at home because I see her. I have been in town but a month, and I lost one place already for believing my own eyes. 30

MR. SEALAND.

Why, sirrah! Have you learnt to lie already?

DANIEL.

Ah, master, things that are lies in the country are not lies at London—I begin to know my business a little better than so. But an you please to walk in, I'll call a gentlewoman to you that can tell you for certain; she can make bold to ask my lady herself. 35

MR. SEALAND.

O, then, she is within, I find, though you dare not say so.

DANIEL.

Nay, nay! That's neither here nor there. What's matter whether she is within or no if she has not a mind to see any-body? 40

MR. SEALAND.

I can't tell, sirrah, whether you are arch or simple, but how-ever get me a direct answer and here's a shilling for you.

DANIEL.

Will you please to walk in? I'll see what I can do for you.

MR. SEALAND.

I see you will be fit for your business in time, child. But I expect to meet with nothing but extraordinaries in such a house. 45

DANIEL.

Such a house! Sir, you han't seen it yet. Pray walk in.

MR. SEALAND.

Sir, I'll wait upon you. *Exeunt.*

30. I] *O1–2, D1*; *om. O3.*

[V.iii] *Scene, Indiana's house. Enter* Isabella.

ISABELLA.
What anxiety do I feel for this poor creature! What will be the end of her? Such a languishing, unreserved passion for a man that at last must certainly leave or ruin her, and perhaps both! Then the aggravation of the distress is that she does not believe he will—not but, I must own, if they are 5
both what they would seem, they are made for one another as much as Adam and Eve were, for there is no other of their kind but themselves.

Enter Daniel.

So, Daniel! What news with you?

DANIEL.
Madam, there's a gentleman below would speak with my 10
lady.

ISABELLA.
Sirrah, don't you know Mr. Bevil yet?

DANIEL.
Madam, 'tis not the gentleman who comes every day and asks for you and won't go in till he knows whether you are with her or no. 15

ISABELLA [*aside*].
Ha! That's a particular I did not know before. —Well! Be it who it will, let him come up to me.

Exit Daniel *and re-enters with* Mr. Sealand. Isabella *looks amazed.*

MR. SEALAND.
Madam, I can't blame your being a little surprised to see a perfect stranger make a visit and—

ISABELLA.
I am indeed surprised! [*Aside.*] I see he does not know me. 20

MR. SEALAND.
You are very prettily lodged here, madam; in troth, you seem to have everything in plenty. (*Aside, and looking about.*) A thousand a year, I warrant you, upon this pretty nest of rooms, and the dainty one within them.

ISABELLA (*apart*).
Twenty years, it seems, have less effect in the alteration of a 25
man of thirty than of a girl of fourteen; he's almost still the

same. But alas! I find, by other men as well as himself, I am not what I was. As soon as he spoke, I was convinced 'twas he. How shall I contain my surprise and satisfaction? He must not know me yet. 30

MR. SEALAND.

Madam, I hope I don't give you any disturbance, but there is a young lady here with whom I have a particular business to discourse, and I hope she will admit me to that favor.

ISABELLA.

Why, sir, have you had any notice concerning her? I wonder who could give it you. 35

MR. SEALAND.

That, madam, is fit only to be communicated to herself.

ISABELLA.

Well, sir, you shall see her. [*Aside.*] I find he knows nothing yet nor shall from me. I am resolved I will observe this interlude, this sport of nature and of fortune. —You shall see her presently, sir; for now I am as a mother and 40 will trust her with you. *Exit.*

MR. SEALAND.

As a mother! Right; that's the old phrase for one of those commode ladies who lend out beauty for hire to young gentlemen that have pressing occasions. But here comes the precious lady herself. In troth, a very sightly woman— 45

Enter Indiana.

INDIANA.

I am told, sir, you have some affair that requires your speaking with me.

MR. SEALAND.

Yes, madam. There came to my hands a bill drawn by Mr. Bevil which is payable tomorrow, and he, in the intercourse of business, sent it to me, who have cash of his, and desired 50 me to send a servant with it, but I have made bold to bring you the money myself.

INDIANA.

Sir, was that necessary?

MR. SEALAND.

No, madam; but, to be free with you, the fame of your

---

43. *commode*] accommodating.

beauty and the regard which Mr. Bevil is a little too well known to have for you excited my curiosity. 55

INDIANA.

Too well known to have for me! Your sober appearance, sir, which my friend described, made me expect no rudeness or absurdity at least—who's there? Sir, if you pay the money to a servant, 'twill be as well. 60

MR. SEALAND.

Pray, madam, be not offended. I came hither on an innocent, nay a virtuous design; and, if you will have patience to hear me, it may be as useful to you, as you are in a friendship with Mr. Bevil, as to my only daughter, whom I was this day disposing of. 65

INDIANA.

You make me hope, sir, I have mistaken you; I am composed again. Be free, say on— (*aside*) what I am afraid to hear—

MR. SEALAND.

I feared, indeed, an unwarranted passion here, but I did not think it was in abuse of so worthy an object, so accomplished a lady as your sense and mien bespeak. But the youth of our age care not what merit and virtue they bring to shame, so they gratify— 70

INDIANA.

Sir, you are going into very great errors. But, as you are pleased to say you see something in me that has changed, at least, the color of your suspicions, so has your appearance altered mine and made me earnestly attentive to what has any way concerned you to inquire into my affairs and character. 75

MR. SEALAND [*aside*].

How sensibly, with what an air she talks! 80

INDIANA.

Good sir, be seated, and tell me tenderly—keep all your suspicions concerning me alive that you may in a proper and prepared way—acquaint me why the care of your daughter obliges a person of your seeming worth and fortune to be thus inquisitive about a wretched, helpless, friendless— (*Weeping.*) But I beg your pardon—though I am an orphan, your child is not; and your concern for her, it seems, has brought you hither. I'll be composed. Pray go on, sir. 85

MR. SEALAND.

How could Mr. Bevil be such a monster to injure such a woman? 90

INDIANA.

No, sir, you wrong him. He has not injured me; my support is from his bounty.

MR. SEALAND.

Bounty! When gluttons give high prices for delicates, they are prodigious bountiful.

INDIANA.

Still, still you will persist in that error. But my own fears tell 95 me all: you are the gentleman, I suppose, for whose happy daughter he is designed a husband by his good father, and he has, perhaps, consented to the overture. He was here this morning dressed beyond his usual plainness, nay, most sumptuously, and he is to be, perhaps, this night a bride- 100 groom.

MR. SEALAND.

I own he was intended such. But, madam, on your account I have determined to defer my daughter's marriage till I am satisfied from your own mouth of what nature are the obligations you are under to him. 105

INDIANA.

His actions, sir, his eyes have only made me think he designed to make me the partner of his heart. The goodness and gentleness of his demeanor made me misinterpret all. 'Twas my own hope, my own passion, that deluded me. He never made one amorous advance to me. His large heart and 110 bestowing hand have only helped the miserable. Nor know I why but from his mere delight in virtue that I have been his care, the object on which to indulge and please himself with pouring favors.

MR. SEALAND.

Madam, I know not why it is, but I, as well as you, am me- 115 thinks afraid of entering into the matter I came about; but 'tis the same thing as if we had talked never so distinctly— he ne'er shall have a daughter of mine.

---

93. *delicates*] delicacies.

INDIANA.

If you say this from what you think of me, you wrong yourself and him. Let not me, miserable though I may be, do injury to my benefactor. No, sir, my treatment ought rather to reconcile you to his virtues. If to bestow, without a prospect of return, if to delight in supporting what might, perhaps, be thought an object of desire with no other view than to be her guard against those who would not be so disinterested, if these actions, sir, can in a careful parent's eye commend him to a daughter, give yours, sir, give her to my honest, generous Bevil. What have I to do but sigh, and weep, to rave, run wild, a lunatic in chains, or, hid in darkness, mutter in distracted starts and broken accents my strange, strange story! 120 125 130

MR. SEALAND.

Take comfort, madam.

INDIANA.

All my comfort must be to expostulate in madness, to relieve with frenzy my despair, and, shrieking, to demand of fate why—why was I born to such variety of sorrows? 135

MR. SEALAND.

If I have been the least occasion—

INDIANA.

No, 'twas Heaven's high will I should be such—to be plundered in my cradle! Tossed on the seas! And even there, an infant captive! To lose my mother, hear but of my father! To be adopted! Lose my adopter! Then plunged again in worse calamities! 140

MR. SEALAND.

An infant captive!

INDIANA.

Yet then to find the most charming of mankind once more to set me free from what I thought the last distress, to load me with his services, his bounties, and his favors; to support my very life in a way that stole at the same time my very soul itself from me. 145

MR. SEALAND.

And has young Bevil been this worthy man?

INDIANA.

Yet then again, this very man to take another! Without

leaving me the right, the pretense of easing my fond heart 150
with tears! For oh, I can't reproach him, though the same
hand that raised me to this height now throws me down the
precipice.

MR. SEALAND.

Dear lady! Oh, yet one moment's patience. My heart grows
full with your affliction. But yet, there's something in your 155
story that—

INDIANA.

My portion here is bitterness and sorrow.

MR. SEALAND.

Do not think so. Pray answer me, does Bevil know your name
and family?

INDIANA.

Alas, too well! Oh, could I be any other thing than what I 160
am—I'll tear away all traces of my former self, my little
ornaments, the remains of my first state, the hints of what I
ought to have been—

In her disorder she throws away a bracelet, which Mr. Sealand *takes up, and looks earnestly on it.*

MR. SEALAND.

Ha! What's this? My eyes are not deceived? It is, it is the
same! The very bracelet which I bequeathed my wife at our 165
last mournful parting.

INDIANA.

What said you, sir? Your wife! Whither does my fancy carry
me? What means this unfelt motion at my heart? And yet
again my fortune but deludes me, for if I err not, sir, your
name is Sealand, but my lost father's name was— 170

MR. SEALAND.

Danvers! Was it not?

INDIANA.

What new amazement! That is indeed my family.

MR. SEALAND.

Know then, when my misfortunes drove me to the Indies,
for reasons too tedious now to mention, I changed my name
of Danvers into Sealand. 175

164. deceived?] deceiv'd? *O1–2*; deceiv'd: *O3*; deceiv'd! *D7*.

Enter Isabella.

ISABELLA.

If yet there wants an explanation of your wonder, examine well this face—yours, sir, I well remember—gaze on, and read, in me, your sister Isabella!

MR. SEALAND.

My sister!

ISABELLA.

But here's a claim more tender yet—your Indiana, sir, your long lost daughter. 180

MR. SEALAND.

Oh, my child! My child!

INDIANA.

All-gracious Heavens! Is it possible? Do I embrace my father?

MR. SEALAND.

And do I hold thee—these passions are too strong for utterance—rise, rise, my child, and give my tears their way— 185
Oh, my sister! *Embracing her.*

ISABELLA.

Now, dearest niece, my groundless fears, my painful cares no more shall vex thee. If I have wronged thy noble lover with too hard suspicions, my just concern for thee, I hope, will plead my pardon. 190

MR. SEALAND.

Oh! Make him then the full amends and be yourself the messenger of joy. Fly this instant! Tell him all these wondrous turns of Providence in his favor! Tell him I have now a daughter to bestow which he no longer will decline, that this day he still shall be a bridegroom, nor shall a fortune, the merit which his father seeks, be wanting. Tell him the reward of all his virtues waits on his acceptance. 195

Exit Isabella.

My dearest Indiana! *Turns, and embraces her.*

INDIANA.

Have I then at last a father's sanction on my love? His bounteous hand to give and make my heart a present worthy of Bevil's generosity? 200

MR. SEALAND.

Oh my child! How are our sorrows past o'erpaid by such a meeting! Though I have lost so many years of soft paternal

dalliance with thee, yet, in one day, to find thee thus, and 205
thus bestow thee in such perfect happiness is ample, ample
reparation! And yet again the merit of thy lover—

INDIANA.

Oh! Had I spirits left to tell you of his actions, how strongly
filial duty has suppressed his love, and how concealment
still has doubled all his obligations, the pride, the joy of his 210
alliance, sir, would warm your heart as he has conquered
mine.

MR. SEALAND.

How laudable is love when born of virtue! I burn to embrace him—

INDIANA.

See, sir, my aunt already has succeeded and brought him to 215
your wishes.

Enter Isabella, *with* Sir John Bevil, Bevil Junior, Mrs. Sealand, Cimberton, Myrtle, *and* Lucinda.

SIR JOHN BEVIL (*entering*).

Where? Where's this scene of wonder? Mr. Sealand, I congratulate, on this occasion, our mutual happiness. Your
good sister, sir, has, with the story of your daughter's fortune, filled us with surprise and joy. Now all exceptions are 220
removed. My son has now avowed his love and turned all
former jealousies and doubts to approbation, and, I am
told, your goodness has consented to reward him.

MR. SEALAND.

If, sir, a fortune equal to his father's hopes can make this
object worthy his acceptance. 225

BEVIL JUNIOR.

I hear your mention, sir, of fortune with pleasure only as it
may prove the means to reconcile the best of fathers to my
love. Let him be provident, but let me be happy. —My ever-destined, my acknowledged wife! *Embracing* Indiana.

INDIANA.

Wife! Oh, my ever loved, my lord, my master! 230

SIR JOHN BEVIL [*to* Indiana].

I congratulate myself as well as you that I had a son who
could, under such disadvantages, discover your great merit.

MR. SEALAND.

Oh, Sir John, how vain, how weak is human prudence!

What care, what foresight, what imagination could contrive such blest events to make our children happy as 235 Providence in one short hour has laid before us?

CIMBERTON (*to* Mrs. Sealand).

I am afraid, madam, Mr. Sealand is a little too busy for our affair. If you please, we'll take another opportunity.

MRS. SEALAND.

Let us have patience, sir.

CIMBERTON.

But we make Sir Geoffry wait, madam. 240

MYRTLE.

Oh, sir! I am not in haste.

During this, Bevil Junior *presents* Lucinda *to* Indiana.

MR. SEALAND.

But here! Here's our general benefactor. Excellent young man that could be at once a lover to her beauty and a parent to her virtue.

BEVIL JUNIOR.

If you think that an obligation, sir, give me leave to overpay 245 myself in the only instance that can now add to my felicity, by begging you to bestow this lady on Mr. Myrtle.

MR. SEALAND.

She is his without reserve; I beg he may be sent for. Mr. Cimberton, notwithstanding you never had my consent, yet there is, since I last saw you, another objection to your 250 marriage with my daughter.

CIMBERTON.

I hope, sir, your lady has concealed nothing from me.

MR. SEALAND.

Troth, sir, nothing but what was concealed from myself—another daughter, who has an undoubted title to half my estate. 255

CIMBERTON.

How, Mr. Sealand! Why then if half Mrs. Lucinda's fortune is gone, you can't say that any of my estate is settled upon her. I was in treaty for the whole, but if that is not to be come at, to be sure, there can be no bargain. Sir, I have nothing to do but to take my leave of your good lady, my 260 cousin, and beg pardon for the trouble I have given this old gentleman.

MYRTLE.

That you have, Mr. Cimberton, with all my heart.

Discovers himself.

OMNES.

Mr. Myrtle!

MYRTLE.

And I beg pardon of the whole company that I assumed the 265
person of Sir Geoffry only to be present at the danger of this
lady's being disposed of and in her utmost exigence to assert
my right to her. Which if her parents will ratify, as they
once favored my pretensions, no abatement of fortune shall
lessen her value to me. 270

LUCINDA.

Generous man!

MR. SEALAND.

If, sir, you can overlook the injury of being in treaty with
one who as meanly left her as you have generously asserted
your right in her, she is yours.

LUCINDA.

Mr. Myrtle, though you have ever had my heart, yet now I 275
find I love you more because I bring you less.

MYRTLE.

We have much more than we want, and I am glad any event
has contributed to the discovery of our real inclinations to
each other.

MRS. SEALAND (*aside*).

Well! However I'm glad the girl's disposed of any way. 280

BEVIL JUNIOR.

Myrtle! No longer rivals now, but brothers.

MYRTLE.

Dear Bevil! You are born to triumph over me! But now our
competition ceases. I rejoice in the pre-eminence of your
virtue and your alliance adds charms to Lucinda.

SIR JOHN BEVIL.

Now, ladies and gentlemen, you have set the world a fair 285
example. Your happiness is owing to your constancy and
merit, and the several difficulties you have struggled with
evidently show

Whate'er the generous mind itself denies
The secret care of Providence supplies. *Exeunt.* 290

EPILOGUE

Spoken by Mrs. Oldfield

Now, I presume, our moralizing knight
Is heartily convinced my sense was right:
  I told him, flat, his Conscious Lovers' passion
Had, many ages past, been out of fashion.
That all attempts to mend the mode were shallow, 5
Our man in favor now's a pretty fellow
That talks and laughs and sings, fights, dances, dresses,
Rakes with an air, and keeps his string of misses,
Then to his fame such courage too belongs
That when by rivals called to account for wrongs, 10
Ne'er stands to talk but—hah—whips 'em through the lungs.
  Not like his Bevil—coolly waits his season,
And traps determined courage into reason;
Nor loves like him, poor soul, confined to one!
And is at vast expense—for nothing done! 15
To pass whole days alone and never meddle,
Treat her with senseless solo—on the fiddle!
And all this chaste restraint, forsooth, to flow
From strait obedience to a father due!
T'have shown his modern breeding, he should rather 20
Not have obeyed, but bit the put, his father;
Or, in compliance to his daddy's courting,
Have starved his dear, and fairly took the fortune.
But to maintain her, and not let her know it—
Oh! the wild—crack-brained notions of a poet! 25
What though his hero never loved before,
He might have, sure, done less for her—or more.
  With scenes of this coarse kind, he owns that plays
Too often have beguiled you of your praise:
Where sense and virtue were allowed no part, 30
That only touched the loose and wanton heart.
If then a diff'rent way of thinking might
Incline the chaste to hear, the learned to write,
On you it rests—to make your profit your delight.

The text is from the second edition of Benjamin Victor, *An Epistle to Sir Richard Steele* (London, 1722), Sig. [A] 2–2v.

This epilogue, never before published with the play, was spoken the first night.

21. *bit*] deceived. 21. *put*] blockhead.

EPILOGUE

By Mr. Welsted
Intended to be Spoken by Indiana

Our author, whom entreaties cannot move,
Spite of the dear coquetry that you love,
Swears he'll not frustrate, so he plainly means,
By a loose epilogue his decent scenes.
Is it not, sirs, hard fate I meet today, 5
To keep me rigid still beyond the play?
And yet I'm saved a world of pains that way.
I now can look, I now can move at ease,
Nor need I torture these poor limbs to please;
Nor with the hand or foot attempt surprise, 10
Nor wrest my features, nor fatigue my eyes.
Bless me! What freakish gambols have I played!
What motions tried and wanton looks betrayed!
Out of pure kindness all! to over-rule
The threatened hiss, and screen some scribbling fool. 15
With more respect I'm entertained tonight:
Our author thinks I can with ease delight.
My artless looks while modest graces arm,
He says, I need but to appear, and charm.
A wife so formed, by these examples bred, 20
Pours joy and gladness 'round the marriage bed;
Soft source of comfort, kind relief from care,
And 'tis her least perfection to be fair.
The nymph with Indiana's worth who vies
A nation will behold with Bevil's eyes. 25

This epilogue was substituted for Victor's in the published play.

Appendix

Chronology

Approximate dates are indicated by *, occurrences in doubt by (?). Dates for plays are those on which they were first made public, either on stage or in print.

Political and Literary Events	*Life and Major Works of Steele*
1631 Death of Donne. John Dryden born.	
1633 Samuel Pepys born.	
1635 Sir George Etherege born.*	
1640 Aphra Behn born.*	
1641 William Wycherley born.*	
1642 First Civil War began (ended 1646). Theaters closed by Parliament. Thomas Shadwell born.*	
1648 Second Civil War. Nathaniel Lee born.*	
1649 Execution of Charles I.	
1650 Jeremy Collier born.	
1651 Hobbes' *Leviathan* published.	
1652 First Dutch War began (ended 1654). Thomas Otway born.	

1656

D'Avenant's *THE SIEGE OF RHODES* performed at Rutland House.

1657

John Dennis born.

1658

Death of Oliver Cromwell.

D'Avenant's *THE CRUELTY OF THE SPANIARDS IN PERU* performed at the Cockpit.

1660

Restoration of Charles II.

Theatrical patents granted to Thomas Killigrew and Sir William D'Avenant, authorizing them to form, respectively, the King's and the Duke of York's Companies.

Pepys began his diary.

1661

Cowley's *THE CUTTER OF COLEMAN STREET.*

D'Avenant's *THE SIEGE OF RHODES* (expanded to two parts).

1662

Charter granted to the Royal Society.

1663

Dryden's *THE WILD GALLANT.*

Tuke's *THE ADVENTURES OF FIVE HOURS.*

1664

Sir John Vanbrugh born.

Dryden's *THE RIVAL LADIES.*

Dryden and Howard's *THE INDIAN QUEEN.*

Etherege's *THE COMICAL REVENGE.*

1665

Second Dutch War began (ended 1667).

Great Plague.
Dryden's *THE INDIAN EMPEROR.*
Orrery's *MUSTAPHA.*

1666
Fire of London.
Death of James Shirley.

1667
Jonathan Swift born.
Milton's *Paradise Lost* published.
Sprat's *The History of the Royal Society* published.
Dryden's *SECRET LOVE.*

1668
Death of D'Avenant.
Dryden made Poet Laureate.
Dryden's *An Essay of Dramatic Poesy* published.
Shadwell's *THE SULLEN LOVERS.*

1669
Pepys terminated his diary.
Susannah Centlivre born.

1670
William Congreve born.
Dryden's *THE CONQUEST OF GRANADA*, Part I.

1671
Dorset Garden Theatre (Duke's Company) opened.
Colley Cibber born.
Milton's *Paradise Regained* and *Samson Agonistes* published.
Dryden's *THE CONQUEST OF GRANADA*, Part II.
THE REHEARSAL, by the Duke of Buckingham and others.
Wycherley's *LOVE IN A WOOD.*

1672
Third Dutch War began (ended 1674).
Joseph Addison born.
Dryden's *MARRIAGE À LA MODE.*

Richard Steele born in St. Bride's parish, Dublin.

1674
New Drury Lane Theatre (King's Company) opened.
Death of Milton.
Nicholas Rowe born.
Thomas Rymer's *Reflections on Aristotle's Treatise of Poesy* (translation of Rapin) published.

1675
Dryden's *AURENG-ZEBE.*
Wycherley's *THE COUNTRY WIFE.**

1676
Etherege's *THE MAN OF MODE.*
Otway's *DON CARLOS.*
Shadwell's *THE VIRTUOSO.*
Wycherley's *THE PLAIN DEALER.*

1677
Rymer's *Tragedies of the Last Age Considered* published.
Aphra Behn's *THE ROVER.*
Dryden's *ALL FOR LOVE.*
Lee's *THE RIVAL QUEENS.*

1678
Popish Plot.
George Farquhar born.
Bunyan's *Pilgrim's Progress* (Part I) published.

1679
Exclusion Bill introduced.
Death of Thomas Hobbes.
Death of Roger Boyle, Earl of Orrery.
Charles Johnson born.

1680
Death of Samuel Butler.
Death of John Wilmot, Earl of Rochester.
Dryden's *THE SPANISH FRIAR.*
Lee's *LUCIUS JUNIUS BRUTUS.*
Otway's *THE ORPHAN.*

1681	
Charles II dissolved Parliament at Oxford.	
Dryden's *Absalom and Achitophel* published.	
Tate's adaptation of *KING LEAR*.	
1682	
The King's and the Duke of York's Companies merged into the United Company.	
Dryden's *The Medal*, *MacFlecknoe*, and *Religio Laici* published.	
Otway's *VENICE PRESERVED*.	
1683	
Rye House Plot.	Moved to Fulham, London, with foster-parents, Henry and Katherine Gascoigne.*
Death of Thomas Killigrew.	
Crowne's *CITY POLITIQUES*.	
1684	Admitted to Charterhouse (school), London.
1685	
Death of Charles II; accession of James II.	
Revocation of the Edict of Nantes.	
The Duke of Monmouth's Rebellion.	
Death of Otway.	
John Gay born.	
Crowne's *SIR COURTLY NICE*.	
Dryden's *ALBION AND ALBANIUS*.	
1687	
Death of the Duke of Buckingham.	
Dryden's *The Hind and the Panther* published.	
Newton's *Principia* published.	
1688	
The Revolution.	
Alexander Pope born.	
Shadwell's *THE SQUIRE OF ALSATIA*.	
1689	
The War of the League of Augsburg began (ended 1697).	Admitted to Christ Church, Oxford, December 21.

Toleration Act. Death of Aphra Behn. Shadwell made Poet Laureate. Dryden's *DON SEBASTIAN.* Shadwell's *BURY FAIR.*	
1690 Battle of the Boyne. Locke's *Two Treatises of Government* and *An Essay Concerning Human Understanding* published.	
1691 Death of Etherege.* Langbaine's *An Account of the English Dramatic Poets* published.	Appointed postmaster (i.e., scholar) of Merton College, August.
1692 Death of Lee. Death of Shadwell. Tate made Poet Laureate.	Left Oxford without a degree, joined Duke of Ormonde's Second Troop of Life Guards, for campaigns of 1692 and 1694 on the Continent(?).
1693 George Lillo born.* Rymer's *A Short View of Tragedy* published. Congreve's *THE OLD BACHELOR.*	
1694 Death of Queen Mary. Southerne's *THE FATAL MARRIAGE.*	
1695 Group of actors led by Thomas Betterton left Drury Lane and established a new company at Lincoln's Inn Fields. Congreve's *LOVE FOR LOVE.* Southerne's *OROONOKO.*	Transferred to Coldstream Guards.*
1696 Cibber's *LOVE'S LAST SHIFT.* Vanbrugh's *THE RELAPSE.*	
1697 Treaty of Ryswick ended the War of the League of Augsburg.	Commissioned ensign (with brevet rank of captain).

Charles Macklin born.
Congreve's *THE MOURNING BRIDE.*
Vanbrugh's *THE PROVOKED WIFE.*

1698

Collier controversy started with the publication of *A Short View of the Immorality and Profaneness of the English Stage.*

1699

Farquhar's *THE CONSTANT COUPLE.*

1700

Death of Dryden.
Blackmore's *Satire against Wit* published.
Congreve's *THE WAY OF THE WORLD.*

Duel with [Henry?] Kelly.

1701

Act of Settlement.
War of the Spanish Succession began (ended 1713).
Death of James II.
Rowe's *TAMERLANE.*

The Christian Hero published.
THE FUNERAL produced at Drury Lane.

1702

Death of William III; accession of Anne.
The Daily Courant began publication.
Cibber's *SHE WOULD AND SHE WOULD NOT.*

Commissioned captain, Thirty-Fourth Foot, on duty at Landguard Fort, Suffolk.

1703

Death of Samuel Pepys.
Rowe's *THE FAIR PENITENT.*

THE LYING LOVER produced at Drury Lane (published January, 1704).

1704

Capture of Gibraltar; Battle of Blenheim.
Defoe's *The Review* began publication (1704–1713).
Swift's *A Tale of a Tub* and *The Battle of the Books* published.

Cibber's *THE CARELESS HUSBAND.*	
1705	
Haymarket Theatre opened.	Resigned from army.*
	Married Margaret Ford Stretch, an heiress.
	THE TENDER HUSBAND produced at Drury Lane.
1706	
Battle of Ramillies.	Death of first wife.
Farquhar's *THE RECRUITING OFFICER.*	Steele appointed Gentleman-Waiter to Queen's husband, Prince George.
1707	
Union of Scotland and England.	Appointed editor of *The London Gazette.*
Death of Farquhar.	
Henry Fielding born.	Married Mary Scurlock.
Farquhar's *THE BEAUX' STRATAGEM.*	
1708	
Downes' *Roscius Anglicanus* published.	
1709	
Samuel Johnson born.	*The Tatler* begun.
Rowe's edition of Shakespeare published.	
Centlivre's *THE BUSY BODY.*	
1710	
	Appointed Commissioner of the Stamp Office.
	Resigned from *Gazette.*
1711	
Shaftesbury's *Characteristics* published.	*The Tatler* terminated (January), *The Spectator,* with Addison, begun (March).
Pope's *An Essay on Criticism* published.	
1712	
	The Spectator (original series) terminated.
1713	
Treaty of Utrecht ended the War of the Spanish Succession.	*The Guardian.*
Addison's *CATO.*	Steele elected to Parliament for Stockbridge, Hampshire.
	The Englishman begun (October).

1714	
Death of Anne; accession of George I. John Rich assumed management of Lincoln's Inn Fields. Centlivre's *THE WONDER: A WOMAN KEEPS A SECRET.* Rowe's *JANE SHORE.*	Political tract, *The Crisis.* *The Englishman* terminated. Expelled from House of Commons on charge of sedition (March). Appointed governor of Drury Lane Theatre (October).
1715	
Jacobite Rebellion. Death of Tate. Rowe made Poet Laureate. Death of Wycherley.	Elected Member of Parliament for Boroughbridge, Yorkshire (February). Knighted by King George I. *The Englishman*, second series (July–November).
1716	
Addison's *THE DRUMMER.*	Appointed Commissioner of the Forfeited Estates for Scotland.
1717	
David Garrick born. Cibber's *THE NON-JUROR.* Gay, Pope, and Arbuthnot's *THREE HOURS AFTER MARRIAGE.*	
1718	
Death of Rowe. Centlivre's *A BOLD STROKE FOR A WIFE.*	Death of Lady Steele; burial in Westminster Abbey.
1719	
Death of Addison. Defoe's *Robinson Crusoe* published. Young's *BUSIRIS, KING OF EGYPT.*	
1720	
South Sea Bubble. Samuel Foote born. Little Theatre in the Haymarket opened. Hughes' *THE SIEGE OF DAMASCUS.*	*The Theatre* (periodical). Suspended as governor of Drury Lane.
1721	
Walpole became first Minister.	Restored to Drury Lane.

1722	
	THE CONSCIOUS LOVERS produced at Drury Lane. Elected Member for Wendover, Buckinghamshire.
1723 Death of Susannah Centlivre. Death of D'Urfey.	
1724	
	Retired to Wales.
1725 Pope's edition of Shakespeare published.	
1726 Death of Jeremy Collier. Death of Vanbrugh. Law's *Unlawfulness of Stage Entertainments* published. Swift's *Gulliver's Travels* published.	
1727 Death of George I; accession of George II. Death of Sir Isaac Newton. Arthur Murphy born.	
1728 Pope's *The Dunciad* (first version) published. Cibber's *THE PROVOKED HUSBAND* (expansion of Vanbrugh's fragment *A JOURNEY TO LONDON*). Gay's *THE BEGGAR'S OPERA.*	
1729	
Goodman's Fields Theatre opened. Death of Congreve. Edmund Burke born.	Death, burial at Carmarthen, Wales.
1730 Cibber made Poet Laureate. Oliver Goldsmith born. Thomson's *The Seasons* published. Fielding's *THE AUTHOR'S FARCE.*	

Fielding's *TOM THUMB* (revised as *THE TRAGEDY OF TRAGEDIES*, 1731).

1731
Death of Defoe.
Fielding's *THE GRUB-STREET OPERA*.
Lillo's *THE LONDON MERCHANT*.

1732
Covent Garden Theatre opened.
Death of Gay.
George Colman the elder born.
Fielding's *THE COVENT GARDEN TRAGEDY*.
Fielding's *THE MODERN HUSBAND*.
Charles Johnson's *CAELIA*.

1733
Pope's *An Essay on Man* (Epistles I–III) published (Epistle IV, 1734).

1734
Death of Dennis.
The Prompter began publication (1734–1736).
Theobald's edition of Shakespeare published.
Fielding's *DON QUIXOTE IN ENGLAND*.

1736
Fielding led the "Great Mogul's Company of Comedians" at the Little Theatre in the Haymarket (1736–1737).
Fielding's *PASQUIN*.
Lillo's *FATAL CURIOSITY*.

1737
The Stage Licensing Act.
Dodsley's *THE KING AND THE MILLER OF MANSFIELD*.
Fielding's *THE HISTORICAL REGISTER FOR 1736*.